MW00476587

JEWELED

Sparkle on!

JEWELED

+ *a sparkling memoir* +

tali nay

corner
chapter
press

JEWELED
Copyright © 2014 Tali Nay

All rights reserved. No part of this book may be reproduced
(except for inclusion in reviews), disseminated or utilized in
any form or by any means, electronic or mechanical, including
photocopying, recording, or in any information storage and
retrieval system, or the Internet/World Wide Web without written
permission from the author or publisher.

For further information, please contact
Corner Chapter Press,
PO Box 21752, Cleveland, OH 44121

Book Cover and Interior Design by VMC Art & Design LLC
Author Photo by Charlene Lybbert Photography

Published in the United States of America

ISBN: 978-0-9914986-5-9
LCCN: 2014905671

This book is dedicated to my hometown jewelry store.
For letting me in, for showing me the ropes,
and for always being so sparkly.

author's note

This book is a true account, my only disclaimer—which applies to anything I write about my life—is that my version of truth is limited to my own interpretations of the experiences I've had and the memories they have generated. To quote Judy Blunt, "In sharing stories with others who were there, we discover how inevitably each perspective offers its own, sure version of events. I've long since made my peace with that variety of fiction we call truth."

I'm with Judy.

PS – This book is not chronological. Which, admittedly, is a pain in the ass. So spend a minute shaking your fist at me, then move on.

What I found does the most good is just
to get into a taxi and go to Tiffany's.

Truman Capote
Breakfast at Tiffany's

three bucks,
two bags, one me

I WAS TWENTY-TWO YEARS OLD THE FIRST time I set foot in Manhattan. A small-town girl through and through, the very thought of navigating subway systems and hailing cabs had me completely unnerved. I'd been asked to accompany a work client to a national trade show, and while I loved this particular client the way I might love my own child, the stress of it all had me in pieces. Such that the night before the week-long trip, I found myself crying hysterically in the arms of my boyfriend. Although it wasn't so much crying in his arms as it was crying on his doorstep while awkwardly waiting for him to invite me in, and then crying while standing in his living room watching him nurse a beer. A very functional relationship, clearly.

When he finally left the couch and turned off the television, he went into his room and retrieved a shoe box. *This oughtta be good*, I thought, as I waited for whatever warped interpretation of comfort and encouragement might be headed my way. He opened the box to reveal a few hundred three by five photographs, accumulated over a decade and probably the only trace of sentimentality to be found in his entire house.

After fishing out a few shots of Grand Central Station, he surprisingly began telling stories from his own experiences in the city. He told me to go up to the roof of my hotel, because I would surely never see a better view; to pay attention to the windows in Grand Central Station, because you can actually climb up in the rafters if you are as clever as you are sneaky; and to—above all else— see the magnificent whale suspended from the ceiling at the Museum of Natural History.

Perhaps I was struck by the relative sweetness of him sharing his memories, or perhaps by how emphatically he had recommended the whale. Either way, I latched on. It felt like some sort of symbol, the whale. As if seeing it, taking a picture of it, and ultimately bringing the evidence back to this very shoe box would save our sham of a relationship. And despite the glorious and addicting mayhem that is a trade show, the decadence of the late-night, three-hour dinners, and the history and significance of monuments such as the Statue of Liberty and Ground Zero, I remained fixed on the whale.

On my day off from working the trade show booth, I set out in search of the museum. Having studied the subway maps feverishly the night before, I was fairly confident in my route. Then again, I had been fairly confident when I'd walked into a bookstore off of Times Square—a real live New York City bookstore!—and puzzled after several minutes over how large the Asian section was, not to mention the apparent lack of any other sections. The employees and other customers, all Asian, were undoubtedly amused to see that I'd unknowingly walked into an Asian bookstore. That aside, I'd gotten the hang of things over the three days since the bookstore incident and successfully got myself onto the correct subway train, museum bound. At least I *thought* it was the correct subway train. Until the wall diagram tracking our path showed our little dot moving further away from the city. What the hell? Where were we going? *Queens?*

I got off at the next stop in order to correct the error, and it took almost a half an hour of waiting before I saw the signs posted and realized that the train I needed was not actually running that day. Having wasted precious time and my already thread-bare confidence, I exited the station and hailed the first taxi I saw. Sliding onto the worn back seat, it suddenly occurred to me that I wasn't exactly sure how this was done. I mean, I didn't even have an address. But at the mere mention of the museum, we were off. The whole thing seemed so much easier than trying to battle the utter confusion of the piss-scented subway trains, a fact I stood firmly behind until we arrived at the museum and the driver coughed out my bill. When it only costs a dollar or two to ride, perhaps the scent of piss isn't so bad.

Inside the museum, I paid my admission fee and practically ripped open the exhibit guide, my eyes scanning the words for anything aquatic. It only took a few minutes to find it; the enormous room with various stuffed creatures lining the walls. In the center of it all was the whale. The giant blue whale. The holy grail of my entire trip.

Approaching the railing that would put me as close to the whale as possible, I positioned my camera for the money shot. But since the size of the whale inhibited its ability to be captured whole, the money shot wasn't really working. Shot after shot, I couldn't get it. Determined, I found a new angle and had just re-pressed my eye to the camera lens when, suddenly, everything came into focus. Literally. What was I even doing there? It was just a whale, and I was wasting my time.

I considered for the first time what exactly it was that *I* wanted to do while in New York, and with purposeful stride I left the museum not ten minutes after arriving. Hailing a cab, I knew exactly where I wanted to go.

"Take me to Tiffany's," I told the driver.

This actually caused him to turn around and look at me as if he hadn't understood, which would have been a problem, as I didn't know how to say "diamonds" in any other languages. A weakness I have since remedied.

"The jewelry store?" the driver asked.

"Yes, on Fifth."

And as we pulled out into the mainstream, I caught a rare glimpse of the sky, which—how fitting—was as blue as a robin's egg.

The first thing you have to keep in mind about the flagship Tiffany & Co. store is that it's huge. It's so damn huge that you have to take an elevator between the floors; an elevator equipped with a uniform-wearing, full-time operator who seems surprisingly pleasant given the monotony of his job. And the stomach flutters it must induce. But maybe it doesn't matter what position you hold at Tiffany. Maybe just being a part of such a dazzling corporation makes any task seem glorious. Even if I hadn't read Marjorie Hart's book, I could absolutely believe it. And I'll never forget walking in those doors the first time, almost cowering at the cavernous space inside, then sinking into a plush chair and pulling out my phone to play the "Guess Where I Am?" game with anyone who would appreciate the answer. Which turned out to be one person.

The second thing you have to keep in mind is that

each floor at Tiffany & Co. is like a different world, the craziest and most populated of which is the silver floor. Because, let's be honest, how many people can actually afford a two-carat engagement ring? I certainly couldn't when I showed up in my taxicab that day, the shards of a doomed relationship in tow. I told the elevator operator to deposit me on the second floor, home of the engagement rings, hoping he wouldn't realize that I actually had no legitimate reason to be there. As if the laws of acceptable customer service would ever require one to have access to both a marriageable boyfriend and a trust-fund's worth of cash prior to perusing the cases. Still, I felt slightly fraudulent.

The doors opened to reveal a rather abandoned space filled with fancy furnishings and cases under diamond lights. The rings were spectacular, and when I'd ultimately selected a gorgeous two-carat, $32,000 ring as my favorite, I couldn't help but think of my mother, who's always trying to talk me out of getting a large stone.

"You're a small person. You have small hands," she'll say.

Although the argument that this necessitates a small stone has never made any sense to me.

When I asked to try on the ring, a somewhat plain-looking saleslady in a dark blazer eyed me carefully as she unlocked the case. I don't think she viewed me as being capable of theft, but surely her seasoned eyes knew the real thing when they saw it. And I most certainly was not the real thing. I maintain that large stones look even *more* spectacular on small hands, and I couldn't take my eyes off of the sparkly facets as I rotated my hand back and forth. It was a solitaire set in platinum. It was perfection.

The saleslady knew as well as I did that I wasn't going to buy the ring, but feeling the need to at least assure her that I did have a boyfriend and that my presence there was consequently not entirely out of scope, I said the first thing I could think of.

"My boyfriend would kill me if he knew I were here."

I'd said this to try and make her laugh, or at least forge some type of bond over both the female love of diamonds and the male fear of having to buy them, but she wasn't amused. I'm not entirely sure she even believed that I *had* a boyfriend, but I tried not to let this detract from the satisfaction of what was such a pivotal moment in my life: trying on an engagement ring at Tiffany. I kept the ring on as long as I dared before handing it over and walking back to the elevator with a slightly heavy heart.

Having been almost the only customer on the diamond floor, you'd have thought I didn't exist on the silver floor for all the time it took to finally get my turn at the counter. The place was a mad house. People were swarming cases, bombarding salespeople, and handing over their credit cards at an alarming rate. I knew when I walked in the building that I would not be leaving empty-handed, and since — just like the rest of the masses—silver was all I could afford, I narrowed it down to either a slightly raised sterling ring with a little bit of faceted texture on top or a dainty silver bracelet with a daisyesque flower above the clasp. I was more taken with the bracelet, but it was significantly more expensive than the ring, and I figured I would probably wear the ring more often anyway.

"Enjoy it," the sincere yet obviously harried saleslady said as she handed over my purchase.

I hadn't expected the signature blue box and accompanying bag to come with my measly transaction, so imagine my delight as I traipsed through the streets of New York City that evening, a little blue bag swinging with my step.

Because the third thing to keep in mind about Tiffany & Co. is that it makes you feel like a million bucks. Sure, I had always pictured my coming to own a piece of Tiffany jewelry slightly differently than this. I'd envisioned a diamond, a man buying it, and the price being closer to $32,000 than to $162. And true, the diamond saleslady might have adopted a better attitude about helping me despite her low chances for a sale, and the silver floor might have been less chaotic. But Tiffany is like a ridiculously good-looking man, in that despite any inconvenience or mistreatment, people will still be eager to line up the next time he's shopping around.

Which is why nothing could temper my good spirits or curb the goodwill I felt that evening, knowing everyone who glanced at my blue bag would know exactly where I'd been. *How fancy she is to be shopping at Tiffany*, they must have thought. Although in actuality it was probably something more like, *How unfortunate she is to be buying her own jewelry.* And while they would have had a point, it is simply a fact that there are times in this world when a girl must take matters into her own hands. Make that *onto* her own hands.

Swiss

The interesting thing about this first trip to Tiffany is that I regretted the ring almost instantly. Not that I regretted purchasing something, it was more that I regretted not purchasing the bracelet. I wore the ring faithfully upon my return home, and, granted, it did fill me with glee to glance down at it and remember my trip to the city, the blue box sitting at home on my dresser. But aside from the fact it came from Tiffany, the ring itself was so unremarkable, and the way it raised up made it impractical as an everyday ring. To be honest, it was ugly, and the only reason I'd bought it was because it was affordable. Alas, the ring soon found its way into a velvety slot in my jewelry box and almost always stayed there.

Several years after this first Tiffany visit, I found myself vacationing in Idaho and stopped at a delightful little antique mall. Since the only thing I'm ever really looking for in such places is jewelry, I headed down to the basement level and began glancing over the cases. They had much more jewelry than they had space, and to look in the cases was to look upon literal heaps of necklaces, bracelets, brooches, rings, and earrings all mixed together. Piss-poor presentation, really, but it's just the sort of challenge I relish, because somewhere in that mess, there was bound to be something good.

Amidst the tangled mess of chains and beads, I spotted what looked like a delicate silver bracelet with a flower over the clasp. It reminded me of the Tiffany bracelet, and I asked the decrepit old saleslady to fish it out. Upon taking it from her hands, my eyes immediately searched the inside for an inscription and went wide at what they found: *Tiffany & Co.* There it was. The very bracelet I had passed over all those years ago. It was *the* bracelet, it was unbelievable, and it was selling for pennies.

As I told the story to the saleslady, she became rather emotional.

"You were meant to have this," she quivered.

Standing there at that counter, I had to agree with her. It was fate. I knew it, she knew it, and somewhere out there, Louis Comfort Tiffany knew it.

The obvious moral of the story here is that when choosing between a ring and a bracelet, one should always choose the bracelet. Nothing against rings, but this is simply good business. Unless it is a wedding ring, an anniversary band, or a flat, wide piece of sterling that sits flush with your finger, there's no need to buy a ring. Any ring. Ever. And, more importantly, even if the piece of jewelry you really want is more expensive than a less-glamorous alternative, you should buy it. You'll wear it more, you'll cherish it more, and you'll come much closer to getting your money's worth than you will by buying something cheaper that you ultimately don't like enough to wear often. So the next time a piece of jewelry takes your breath away, don't fuss with the decision. Just tell the salesperson to box it up for you. And then pray to God that it doesn't cost $32,000.

firsts

I DIDN'T KNOW MUCH ABOUT JEWELRY STORES on my first day at Carlton Jewelers. Never having had time for a job while in high school and having stayed away at school the first summer while in college, I was twenty years old by the time I got around to doing what I'd always meant to, which is work at my hometown jewelry store, owned by Steve Carlton.

It was the summer before my final year in college, and although it only paid minimum wage and I didn't even work every day, the job felt like luxury. On that first day, I was awed by the store, the jewels, and the $10 Steve handed me to go down the street and get us all frozen yogurt. I was being *paid* to play with diamonds and eat frozen yogurt? If anything in my life had ever seemed too good to be true, this was it.

Reality set in soon enough as the store manager, Nancy, showed me the ropes. Nancy was somewhere in her forties and had a son and daughter with whom I had gone to high school. She did her job incredibly well, and even on that first day, I wanted Nancy to like me. To be impressed by me. Of course, impressing anyone would have been hard to pull off, since when it came to working in a jewelry store, I didn't know what the hell I was doing.

Take store purchases, which were every bit as complicated as some minor surgeries. Everything was rung up on a computer, tags scanned and customer information entered. If the customer was new, you had to ask them for all their information, which no one really likes giving. What happened to the days when you could anonymously purchase an expensive piece of jewelry without telling people where you live, whether you have a spouse, and getting fliers in the mail about upcoming sales on Antwerp diamonds? After the credit cards have been swiped, a task in itself, receipts print out of both the credit card scanner and the printer. At this point, you will have officially made a sale. And you will have also turned one hundred years old. So congratulations.

My trial-run transaction was a sale to a woman who used to live on the street where I grew up. I had hoped to have the anonymity factor working in my favor, but alas, this woman totally knew who I was. Beautiful and stylish, she had three daughters who were also beautiful and stylish, and she was watching me fumble with the computer keys as I asked for her husband's name, even though I already knew it. It's just a fact that no one wants to be in the presence of anyone they know while in an awkward and vulnerable moment, yet I was in one. And there stood this woman. It reminded me of my first trip to the gynecologist the year before. I was nineteen, away from home, and the receptionist had for some reason felt the need to leave her post at the front desk and open the exam room door (mid-exam, mind you) to stand at my side and hold my hand. Her insistence that I not be alone during my foray into the world of speculums might have been sweet had I been wearing pants.

Up to my ears in things I knew nothing about—like how to actually sell a piece of jewelry—Nancy finally assigned me a task I could handle. The ring that had just been purchased needed to be gift-wrapped, and I took the tiny box over to the wrapping station feeling no small amount of relief. Wrapping paper, tape, scissors. Like I had done every Christmas since I could remember. Perhaps it's because I'd never actually wrapped a box that small, or perhaps I'd done a piss-poor job on every present I'd ever wrapped, but by the time I was done with the ring box, it looked like the work of a kindergartener. A drunk kindergartener. A drunk kindergartner who only had the use of one arm. And was also blind.

I stared at the bulges of excess paper jutting out from the box and wondered if my running away right now would be explainable. Realizing that it probably wasn't, and that I had to bring *something* back to Nancy, I made

my way to the front of the store where she and the customer were waiting. When I handed Nancy the box,
she didn't immediately take it. Rather, she let it sit in my
outstretched hand while she struggled to balance her surprise and disapproval with the professionalism she wanted
to maintain. The customer, after all, was watching.

"Let's….let's just…redo this," she said, feigning
cheerfulness.

And without another word, Nancy disappeared into
the back and returned not two minutes later with a
gloriously-wrapped box, complete with curled ribbons
and a big bow on top. It's worth noting that my own
measly attempt had included neither ribbons nor bows.
We rarely had them at home, and, honestly, using them
hadn't even occurred to me, surrounded by them as I was.

Humiliated beyond expression at my failure with even
such a basic task, perfecting the art of wrapping a jewelry
box became my number one priority. For the next few
days I spent all my spare time wrapping empty boxes. The
key is to not use more paper than you need, and once I
figured out the appropriate amount needed for each box,
the process became as seamless as it was scientific.

I took a few of my creations upstairs to the office of
Steve's wife, Pamela, who I thought to have pretty high
standards and whose approval I desperately sought. I
could not be seen by these people as an idiot.

"What do you think?" I asked as I presented the
wrapped boxes.

"I think someone is a perfectionist," Pamela replied, lightly chiding me for being so concerned about it when my wrapping abilities appeared to be just fine.

Of course, Pamela hadn't seen my original wrapping job, so she didn't understand what a before-and-after moment this truly was. And I didn't want to show Nancy, as I preferred to drop the whole topic of me and gift-wrapping altogether and never give her cause to remember my sloppy debut.

Maybe the first day on any job is always a train wreck. Maybe this was simply the most effective way for the universe to illustrate the principle of practice makes perfect. Or that there's a lot more to jewelry stores than jewelry. All I can tell you for sure is that to this day, my gift-wrapped small boxes are so beautiful, they could bring you to tears. And probably have if you purchased anything from Carlton Jewelers in the summer of 2002. Unless you bought something on my first day.

Classic round

I received my first significant piece of jewelry when I was in the seventh grade. Black Hills gold was all the rage in junior high, and it seemed like all my classmates had some. Looking at it now, it's borderline hideous and exactly the type of jewelry that screams either, "I'm a thirteen-year-old girl," or "I actually *live* in the Black Hills and this here's the damn near prettiest stuff I ever clapped eyes on." But at the time it seemed like the most beautiful and luxurious thing I could ever hope to own, and I always looked at my friends' hands with envy, as they all, without fail, owned a Black Hills gold ring.

I remember Dad taking me to Carlton Jewelers one day to look at rings. Picking out one for us to buy was not the objective of the trip, and I'm sure I knew that going in. I had never been given a piece of jewelry and had no reason to believe I would receive one in the future. But that didn't stop me from wanting to come in and look around whenever I could convince Dad to take me to the jewelry store. It's not that we didn't have any money, but I'm sure my parents, only one of whom ever worked while we kids were growing up, operated on a budget, so we didn't typically receive gifts as expensive and unnecessary as jewelry.

This is why getting a Black Hills gold ring the Christmas I was in seventh grade was about the biggest shock of my life up to that point. I couldn't believe it, and I was immediately smitten. The ring's design was two leaves that were connected to the gold band by two curves, meant to represent vines, and underneath the leaves were four little gold dots, almost like berries.

At a time in life when people's perception of me for

owning jewelry was as important—or more important—
than the jewelry itself, the best part about possessing the
ring was that my friends soon noticed that I owned it. I
didn't even mention it to anyone because I wanted them to
discover it on their own; maybe they'd assume I'd had it all
along and they had simply not realized it. This discovery
did not take long. It may even have been my first school
day with the ring that my friend Sabrina noticed it while
we were in the computer lab.

"When did you get that?" she asked, and I was in
the club.

The Black Hills gold club. Whatever that means.

Over the remainder of my teenage years, there would
occasionally be a little box under the Christmas tree,
one that obviously contained jewelry, and the surprising
thing is that the tag would say, "From Dad." In his own
handwriting and everything. Which meant that Dad,
all on his own, had gone to the jewelry store to buy
something sparkly for his jewelry-loving daughter.

I confess that these gifts, the jewelry from my Dad,
have remained some of the most special to me. Because
even though almost everything I ever got for Christmas
said "From Mom and Dad" on the tag, that pretty much
just meant Mom. I'm sure it's typical the world over for
Moms to be more involved in the Christmas shopping
than Dads. Which is why I loved seeing those little
boxes under the tree so much. I loved picturing Dad
leaving his clinic after a long day at work and stopping

at Carlton's instead of coming straight home. I loved picturing him perusing the cases and selecting something that he thought I would like. I loved knowing that he'd done something special for me all on his own.

On one particular Christmas morning, I remember spotting the little wrapped box immediately. It was wedged deep into the pile of gifts, and I snuck a peek at the tag just to be sure: "To Tali, From Dad." Eureka! I saved it for last, naturally, and when I opened the little box, I had a hard time containing my smile as I fished through the tissue paper to get to the velvet box beneath. When it became apparent that there was no velvet box, it didn't really phase me. It only struck me as odd that whatever was inside—a necklace, perhaps?—was merely draped amongst the tissue paper. When it then became apparent that tissue paper was the *only* thing in the box, I began to panic. I pulled the tissue paper out completely and at the bottom of the box lay only a small strip of paper. On the paper were typed the following five words: *Jesus Christ is my Savior.*

To my Dad's credit, this was certainly an effective lesson on the real meaning of Christmas. Of course, it might have been a bit more well received had the other side of the paper said something like, "Now go to the kitchen where your *real* present is sitting on your placemat at the table." But it didn't. There was no jewelry that year, and to my Dad's point, it really shouldn't have mattered. I already had the best gift I could ever receive, we all did, and I assure you that over the years I have certainly come to appreciate this much more than any piece of jewelry. But I can also assure you that at the time, I didn't give a snit about Christianity. Not if it was the reason why I hadn't gotten any jewelry that morning. Pretty sure I would have gladly exchanged my eternal soul for whatever sparkly thing would have been in that box. Hell can't possibly be that bad if you've got bling.

Royal

I first wore pierced earrings at age ten, and if I recall correctly, which I may not, that in itself was a negotiation. I was initially told I had to wait until I was twelve to get my ears pierced. This seemed horribly unfair, and I'm not sure if my incessant whining is what changed my parents' mind or if they would have softened regardless, but saving me from an extra two pierceless years is among the ever-growing list of things in my life for which I must thank them.

Because without pierced ears, a girl has nowhere to turn except, I shudder to even mention them, clip-on earrings. Women of the world, do you remember these? Do you remember how cool you used to think they were, back when having the look of earrings was better than wearing no earrings at all? Do you also remember how horrid they suddenly seemed once the novelty wore off and you realized you were the only one not yet wearing real earrings?

Not that I can in hindsight give my parents much of a hard time for making me wait, as I wouldn't want to deal with maintaining the ears and earrings of a baby, toddler, or small child any more than they did. Still, twelve seemed extreme to my ten-year-old self, which is why I was delighted when my mom suddenly announced that she would be taking me — in the middle of a school day! — to get my ears pierced.

Sitting in the school hallway waiting for her, I'm embarrassed to admit that I suddenly wondered what I'd gotten myself into. And clip-on earrings looked pretty damn good as I sat in a chair at the mall watching the woman load the gun she was about to shoot into my ear lobes. One at a time, no less! Honestly, I'm surprised there aren't more little girls out there with only one pierced ear.

Once I had my ears pierced, the good news is that it opened up a world of possibilities when it came to the obnoxious, impractical, and ugly earrings that pre-teens love. Of course, this was also the bad news. I began acquiring earrings at an alarming rate, all, in hindsight, the most hideous things you've ever seen. Hearts, flowers, various mixes of fake metals and fake stones, and the bigger and more dangley the better. I can recall a two-inch-long pair of bulky but colorful wooden parrots that were among my favorites, simply because of their sheer size. I mean, just think of it. Two-inch parrots hanging from your ears. Now *that's* impressive.

Almost equally impressive is the type of storage device a person would need to house all these hideous earrings. Mine was a larger–than-life heap of gold that sat on the desk in my room. It was in the shape of three intertwining hearts, and the edges of each heart were littered with holes into which earring backs could be set. It was given to me by a neighbor as a thank you gift for babysitting, and if the goal of a gift is to delight the receiver, this woman could not have nailed it better.

I loved that earring holder almost as much as I loved all those earrings, and the only storage method that could rival that of the three-hearted gold wonder was the set of stackable, circular compartments into which my fisherman father would sort his fly-tying supplies. Feathers and fur and hooks and such. Dad had given me a stack of the compartments, and because I loved organization just as much as jewelry, I would sometimes move my earrings, one pair per circular compartment, into the stack from Dad and keep them in there until the gold hearts beckoned me back.

Of course, the interesting thing about me and earrings is that I was born with a bump on my left earlobe. I've been a bit self-conscious of it throughout my life.

Not only because the bump itself is noticeable, but also because it makes earrings appear uneven when I'm wearing them. Only if a person were really look-ing for that, mind you, but still, it's noticeable. The best I can figure, my left earlobe must have become scrunched in the womb, causing a portion of it to grow out as opposed to down. I'm probably explaining this all wrong, so picture more birthmark and less Elephant Man, but either way, it's something I'm reminded of every time I put on a pair of earrings. Especially two-inch wooden parrots.

Briolette

One of the days I remember most clearly from my teenage years is the day I received my first piece of fine jewelry. Let me first clarify what I mean by fine jewelry, because this was certainly not the first piece of jewelry I had ever received, and I would never want to downplay the awe, glee, and newfound sense of good fortune that settled into my being when my parents presented me with my first official bauble: the Black Hills gold ring that I've mentioned previously and recall most fondly to this day. By fine jewelry I simply mean anything containing precious gem stones, which the aforementioned Black Hills gold ring did not.

I'll preface the story by saying that I had visited my Aunt Leah's house in Washington state the previous summer. It was not an unusual summer occurrence; I spent some time from each of my teenage summers at the small lakefront home of Leah and her husband Wade. It was a treat for several reasons, especially because my cousins Brian, Jared, and Kyle would usually be there too. I could write an entire book about how much fun we had over the years, how much I loved having boy cousins my own age, and how much I've worried over the years about them meaning much more to me than I ever did to them. Suffice it to say, the times that were spent with these boys were among the highlights of my childhood. And in the letter that I wrote to Brian shortly before his death at age twenty-four, that's exactly what I told him.

Time at Aunt Leah's was also a treat because of the lake itself. While I was never a waterskiing enthusiast in those days, I surely would have been had I actually been able to successfully get up out of the water. Requiring nothing more than a thumb and index finger to operate, Sea-Doos were more my style, and having unlimited access to all of this—including a boat, and, more importantly, a dock to repeatedly jump off the end of—it was any kid's summer fantasy. The grassy area before the dock began housed a fire pit where we made s'mores every night. S'mores with enough choc-olate for each of us to have two entire Hershey's bars to ourselves. Did I mention fantasy?

But my favorite thing about Leah's house was Leah herself. The almost paradoxical epitome of both luxury and generosity, she represented everything I wished I was. Not to mention everything I wished I *had*. Beauty, style, career and financial success, hard-working husband, lakefront home, and always a sports car of some kind. I remember a BMW, a Porsche at one point, and I'll never forget the Mercedes, because she may or may not have let me drive it, and I may or may not have almost imme-diately backed it into something while behind the wheel. (I may or may not have been twenty-four years old.)

Everything Leah introduced me to was infinitely fancier and cooler than anything I had, anything I even *knew* about. From the sandwich known as the French Dip—with its own salty dipping sauce that was so yummy I could drink it by the cup full—to the Madonna cassette she smuggled to me and my sister (our parents said we weren't allowed to listen to Madge's music) to fun and sassy words like brouhaha, I couldn't get enough of my Aunt Leah. So you can probably imagine how excited I was when one summer night at her house found us going through a box of some of her things. And my excitement turned to internal hysteria when the box turned out to contain a few pieces of jewelry, one of which caught my eye and had my heart immediately.

It was a ring with a thin gold band and a flower-shaped cluster of stones on top, and it was so very compact and sophisticated that I was transfixed. Speechless. The petals were six tiny rubies arranged around a single diamond, also tiny, and the whole thing was so tasteful and dainty that it had to be the most perfect first piece of fine jewelry a teenager could ever have. It struck me as infinitely more mature than Black Hills gold. To even think about having such a legitimate piece in my own collection—real rubies and diamonds!—was beyond my comprehension. But clearly I was getting ahead of myself. Because while the thought of my somehow coming to own the ring immediately crossed my mind, it didn't belong to me, and I refused to play the part of the annoying niece who nags until she gets what she wants. Nor was I comfortable playing the role of Gollum in the way this story played out.

Still, I was only human. Of the teenage girl variety. And I loved jewelry more than anything else. So it was hard to focus as Leah started to expound on her history with the ring. I vaguely remember her saying in that conversation that the ring may have at one point belonged to another of my aunts. Not one of her actual sisters, but to my Uncle Rick's wife. Which didn't really make any sense. Why would Rick's wife have given the ring to her sister-in-law? Whatever. The thought that consumed me as I half-listened to Leah while gazing obsessively at the ring and hobbling around my dank cave lair on all fours was that she wasn't even using the ring. She kept it in a box. Not a jewelry box, but a regular box. Big, brown, cardboard, and put away in a place she rarely even had cause to look.

For the life of me I couldn't figure out why a person who owned rubies and diamonds wouldn't wear them every moment of every day. It was tough to balance the part of me that knew it was inappropriate to voice these concerns to Leah right there with the part of me that was becoming more convinced by the second that it made more sense for the ring to be mine.

Not wanting to seem overzealous but definitely wanting her to know I was interested, I mentioned the ring as I said goodbye to Leah at the end of the week.

"And if you're ever looking to get rid of that little red ring…," I threw out there without even completing the sentence.

It goes without saying that I thought about the ring many times over the ensuing months. About how perfect it would be in my own collection. About how much I would cherish it. About how much more sense it made on my finger as opposed to a big box in Leah's closet. But most of all, I thought about how foolish I was to think Leah would just hand over a ruby and diamond ring. If *I* had one, I certainly wouldn't be looking to part with it either.

Which is why even when I spotted the small wrapped gift from Leah under the Christmas tree that year, I didn't think it would be the ring. Yes, it would be a perfect gift for me, but it would also be bafflingly generous. Even when I opened the little package to find a jewelry case covered in black velvet, I scarcely allowed myself to hope. Even when I opened the case and saw the ring in all its flower-shaped glory, I couldn't believe it.

I always say I could write a book called *Everything Cool That I Have Came From My Aunt Leah*, and I truthfully could. And still might. But no matter how many things I've received from her before or since, the little red ring tops the list.

Drop

My first and only strand of pearls came from my years in business school. A gift from the MBA program administration, they presented each female student with a strand of pearls and each male student with a silk tie. The administration had just undergone a change, and the new president had a very different style and manner than his predecessor. I wasn't sure I was on board, but then again, the previous president had never given us jewelry.

Because of my jewelry obsession, or maybe because

this is just where our minds go when it comes to pearls, one of my first thoughts after hearing about our impending gifts was, *"Does he mean* real *pearls?"* Because when it comes to value, there is a difference. Obviously. And I was curious about how big of a gift this actually was. How much did we really mean to our administration?

My first clue to the puzzle of the pearls' worth was the value of a silk tie. Surely the administrators would want to parallel the two gifts in terms of worth, but the problem was, and still is, that I have no idea about the worth of a silk tie. Were we talking 100% silk? Was this a precious material for ties? I couldn't be sure, but to me, silk in a tie didn't sound like much of a stretch. It even sounded normal. Expected. And nothing you couldn't get for $24.99 on a clearance rack at the department store. It wasn't looking good for the authenticity of our pearls.

Still though, there was an awful lot of buzz among the girls about this gift. How generous it was, how unexpected. *Can you believe it?? A whole strand of pearls! Just for being students in this program! The magnanimity!* And so I remained hopeful. Surely no group of women would be making such a fuss over pearls unless they were real.

My first clue—although I just said that about the value of a silk tie—really should have been the way the pearls were packaged when they arrived. You can imagine the anticipation with which I'd been waiting for the pearls, and when the day finally came and I saw them being handed out in the MBA lounge, my heart lurched.

The pearls. Are here.

It was all I could do to stay calm.

Even after I saw the pearls as I approached the woman who was handing them out, nothing struck me as fraudulent. And that's saying something. Because the pearls were packaged in clear plastic sleeves. Not resting gently around a neck mold inside a velvet jewelry case, but hanging at their full length inside of narrow plastic sleeves. PLASTIC SLEEVES, people. Flimsy ones. Not unlike the way candy necklaces are packaged. The ones where you bite off the individual pieces. Those same plastic sleeves.

But like I said, the illusion of these being real pearls was still suspended in my mind. In true Fox Mulder style, I wanted to believe. I needed to believe. I needed to believe that I was holding in my hand a string of genuine pearls; that I now had some in my collection. I needed to believe that the administration had not simply bought us cheap knock offs that were packaged like the kiddie knick knacks you could order by the dozen from the East India Trading Company. And so I reasoned with myself that perhaps even real pearls were packaged this way when purchased in bulk. It was possible, right?

Until I actually took a strand, my strand, into my palm and closed my fist around it. And then it was perfectly clear that it was, in fact, *not* possible for fine jewelry to be packaged this way. For the crinkly sound that followed was about the most unholy thing I'd ever heard. The indisputable sound of cheapness. That crinkle gave them away.

I didn't have to look much further after the crinkly packaging. Each pearl had a thick, banded middle with a definite line all the way around, and the two sides that the middle divided were not seamless. They bulged over, such that the pearls were not completely round. They were pretty much butt-shaped. They had the unmistakable look of being somehow put together instead of simply being.

Speaking of fakes, there's something very slippery about the authenticity of pearls. People always want to know if the pearls they come into contact with, own, see, or covet on someone else's neck are "real." This need to know is surely exacerbated by the sheer elegance suggested by a string of pearls. We want to know that we are, in fact, as classy as we think we are.

Because let's review: While it doesn't get fancier than diamonds, you will never get classier than pearls. Think Jackie O. Think of anyone else who's ever been noted for donning them, because they were probably only channeling her.

And let's not forget that pearls are also more rare. Not necessarily in supply (pearl culturing is a huge industry) or our ability to acquire them—a pearl is much more affordable than a diamond. But ask yourself this: Do you actually own any pearls? A pendant maybe, or a pair of post earrings. But how about a full string of shiny whites? When I say rare in this instance, I mean there's a much smaller percent of the population that can actually say yes.

In earlier years I wasn't so concerned with the "realness" of pearls since I couldn't have even told you what made a real pearl in the first place. Words like "freshwater" and "cultured" confused me, and for a long time I assumed that freshwater meant real and cultured meant fake. When I finally learned enough to know that any pearl, cultured or not, that's grown inside a mollusk is real and all others are fake, things made much more sense. The trick then became how to identify whether any given pearl or strand was actually real.

Perhaps the biggest surprise when studying pearls in my gemology training came in a pearl grading lab class. We were learning how to grade pearls on things like color, luster, and nacre quality, and surrounded by stands upon strands of perfect-looking pearls, I wondered why we weren't spending any time discussing how to tell real pearls from fake pearls. Because they aren't all as easy to spot as those on my b-school necklace. I wanted a foolproof way to tell immediately what was what. Real or fake. Genuine or imposter. Yet all we focused on was how to grade the specific attributes and properties of pearls you already know are real, and I remember leaving the class feeling a bit unfulfilled.

As with all jewelry though, it often comes down to

the intent with which something is given or the circumstances surrounding the gift or giver rather than the value or preciousness of the piece itself. Which could explain why I still have my butt pearls and still feel a little awed to hold them even though I know they are fake. They make me feel important, special, pampered. They remind me of a time when I was making great educational strides and preparing to go places I couldn't have imagined. Like, um, Cleveland. They make me feel young, productive, and at my classiest when I have them on. Even though they're shaped like butts.

Scissor

The first time a man bought me jewelry, I was thirty years old. Not that I could blame my boyfriends for always having shied away from this type of purchase. It must be intimidating when faced with the task of buying jewelry for someone with enough opinions about it to write an entire book. Although the real reason none of them ever did probably had more to do with the fact that I was notorious for dating cheap men. Not that I did it on purpose, but they'd always turn out to be stingy.

Then at age thirty I fell in love with a man who was

established in his career, owned his own home, and reveled in thoroughly spoiling his girlfriend. All of which were new to me. If you're wondering who are these cheap, transient, weak-sauce boys I'd spent the previous decade dating, that'll be the subject of a different book. Suffice it to say, it was refreshing to finally find a *man*.

Before I describe the bauble he bought me, let me first confess that I've always had mixed feelings about men picking out jewelry for the women in their lives. Which probably seems inconsistent, since I will vehemently declare in this book that the answer to the question of what to buy a woman is always jewelry. But look at it this way. While jewelry has a higher probability of delighting a woman than almost any other gift, not every woman likes every piece of jewelry.

There are multiple ways to go about selecting your purchase, and the one I recommend if the goal is to make sure it's something she really wants involves a little help on her part. So listen up, ladies. Most jewelry stores are familiar with the idea of a "wish list," so what I'd suggest every woman do is to always have a short list of favorites on file with your local jeweler. Your man can then come in any time and always have a few options of things he knows you'll love.

A second option for deciding on a jewelry purchase is to study her existing collection and deduce from her style what she might like. This is risky, because you might still end up with something she's not crazy about, or it might leave you baffled if you aren't able to pick up on the trends in her current collection. Like, say, if all the stones are emerald cuts, or all the earrings are about the same length. Would you even notice that?

But the most risky of all would be walking into a store and simply picking out something that catches your eye. Something that you think is nice, unique, or perfect for her. *Think.* Meaning you might not be right, and you'd have to hope her love for you would make up the difference if she actually hates it. But this is an interesting point, and one I've been reflecting on over recent years.

See, I'd never actually believed there was any validity to the claim that you could like a piece of jewelry simply because it came from the person you love. I had listened to my mother claim from time to time that she would never even think about exchanging jewelry my dad picked out for her. And this always sounded like crazy talk. Is this really how women prefer to handle situations such as these? Instead of pick out something else that you actually like—or at least like better—you would put up with something you didn't particularly care for just because of who picked it out? Especially when said picker had given you the guilt-free go-ahead to exchange it?

It's not that I didn't like the necklace my Manly McMan boyfriend picked out and gave to me for our first Christmas together. But my first thought when I opened the little jewelry case was, *I would have never picked this out for myself.*

I was surprised, incredibly so, that he'd bought me jewelry in the first place. He'd wrapped it in a bigger box so I wouldn't automatically know that the gift was in the jewelry realm. When I finally got down to the little white jewelry case, the necklace inside bore a dark, round stone with an oval of baby round diamonds fastened just above it. What surprised me so much was the darkness of the stone, because the second thought I had after opening the case was, *What stone is this?* And I was the gemologist!

The stone was so dark it looked black. Only when I held it up and rotated it a bit could I detect a hint of purplish-brown. Still, I was at a loss.

"What stone is this?" I asked.

"You tell me!" he replied.

Not in a way that suggested it was a little test for me, but in a way that suggested he himself had no idea. And it was at this point that the necklace became instantly dear to me.

This man, the man that I loved, had walked into a jewelry store knowing nothing about jewelry. He asked the salesperson to point him in a direction, as even after looking through each case, this still left him clueless as to what ballpark he was in. Hundreds, thousands, millions? How much did all this stuff cost? And then the best part, which is that after establishing which types of things were within the price range he had in mind, *without even knowing what he was buying* he simply picked out what he liked best. The piece he thought was the most beautiful, the most striking.

And for the first time in my life, I understood the effect this has on women. He had picked it out. *He* had. It was the necklace he wanted me to have. That he had made the effort and taken the risk made me all kinds of swoony, and not that I had disliked the necklace at first glance, but I had been skeptical. Because it's possible to interpret *I would have never picked this out for myself* as *I don't like this*. But there's another way of looking at it. A better way. Or at least, in my case, a more accurate way. Because if you would have never picked something out for yourself, then the only way you'll ever come to own it is if someone else picks it out for you. So if someone does, how truly fortunate you are.

The dark stone below the diamonds was a smoky quartz, by the way, and I could have exchanged it for something that was more in line with my other pieces of jewelry, but then I would never have had anything with such deep, rich color. I would never have realized that this opened up many more possibilities with regard to jewelry/outfit pairings in my own closet. In short, I would never have known what I was missing.

As it was, I started wearing the necklace all the time, and I appreciated its uniqueness and variance from the rest of my collection right away. Not to mention it warmed my heart to think of Manly McMan picking it out.

I guess the real test is if he would have gotten me something hideous. Like peridot. I have no idea how far the lover/jewelry bond can carry a person, but I can tell you this: I had a dream once that he proposed with the ugliest ring I had ever seen, and I still said yes. In the words of Ruben Land, make of that what you will.

lessons from the store

SELLING JEWELRY IS A SLOW BUSINESS, PARTIC-
ularly in a small timber town with a generally depressed
economy. While holidays provided decent foot traffic,
on a regular day in the store, you could go hours with no
sales. No customers even. And since I have an inherent
need to be productive while on the clock, I would turn
on these long afternoons to the series of rather useless
chores I saved just for these occasions.

Things like polishing the silver, folding the sheet
boxes so they were ready to be wrapped with purchases,
fanning out each loop of the bows we bought in bulk,
wiping fingerprints off the outsides of cases yet again.
I suppose these chores weren't *totally* useless. I mean,
we did need bows and boxes, but why anyone would
need two dozen of them assembled at any given time
and piled into a mountain over on the little wrapping
table was probably more to the point. And the slightly

depressing thing about doing such tasks was that doing them meant I wouldn't have to do them again for several weeks. So the list of useless chores I could do on the next slow day was now a lot smaller.

It goes without saying that the activity to which I devoted the biggest percentage of my idle hours at Carlton Jewelers was trying to figure out what to buy. For *myself*. I had a measly income working against me, but the much greater element at work was the employee discount on anything I wanted. I'd have been a fool to pass up diamonds at cost. Because what you might but probably don't realize is the diamond markup is easily 300 percent. No need to freak out, because that's pretty standard and people are used to paying it, but my point is that if you ever have the chance to *not* pay it, you should ride that wave as long as is humanly possible.

When it came to listing specific information about a piece of jewelry, including price, Carlton's had the same system that most other stores have. That of a sticky, folded-over white tag adhered somewhere on the item. The tag contained a shorthand description of the item, a small barcode, the total diamond carat weight if it contained diamonds, and the price. But for those in the know, basically just the employees, you could flip the tag over and find one more piece of information: the actual cost. As in how much we paid for it when we bought it from the supplier.

This cost figure was always displayed in codes, no

doubt so that our customers wouldn't catch on and realize how much more than cost they were paying. These codes were very important to me, as they let me know whether obtaining a piece of jewelry was within the realm of possibility. I wasted no time checking the tags on new items in our inventory, and while the codes dashed my hopes to pieces often enough, they also saw me elated on numerous occasions. And once something I liked was discovered to be affordable, it was immediately added to the list of things I planned on buying before the end of the summer.

The vast majority of what I bought each summer was sterling silver. Hell, it's cheap. When I saw a pair of plain zig-zag shaped sterling earrings with the cheapest code I had ever seen, I bought them on the spot. Not because I really liked them all that much, but because I could get them for $3.00. I bought many, many pairs of earrings. Sterling with mother of pearl, sterling with cheap blue topaz, sterling with onyx. Bracelets, mostly sterling, and even one of those at-the-time popular Italian charm bracelets that I filled with charms.

I bought several sterling necklaces, including a few that even came in sets with bracelets. I was particularly taken with the necklaces made up of several thin wires, each wire strung with tiny silver balls of different sizes. One of these sets, in fact, was the only purchase I nearly missed out on. Nancy bought for her daughter the one I was planning to buy for myself. Cursing myself for postponing the purchase, I was crushed until we brought another one in a few weeks later.

My favorite sterling necklace from the Carlton years was a simple box chain that boasted a small dog-tag-like tab of silver. It was such an all-purpose necklace; I loved its simplicity. I loved that the silver tag hung down and would sometimes go under my shirt, like I had a secret worth keeping. I also bought a white gold chain, short, and about the thinnest one you've ever seen. This one I loved because it was like an illusion. Other than the sparkles that reflected when I moved, you could hardly tell I was wearing a necklace at all. Another secret, I suppose.

My biggest lapse in judgment came when I purchased an ankle bracelet. In my defense, I thought they were sexy. Although upon further reflection, I suppose that's not really a defense. Because ankle bracelets are about as sexy as ankle tattoos. They are distracting and juvenile and kind of white trash. Yet I bought one. A white gold one with Black Hills gold leaves on the side. I'm embarrassed to admit that I wore this ankle bracelet for years after I bought it, which put me in my mid-twenties before I realized that no one actually wore ankle bracelets anymore. And no stylish person ever had.

In contrast, the crowning acquisition of my time at Carlton's came in the form of a pair of diamond stud earrings from Antwerp, Belgium. Antwerp has always been a special place in the world of diamonds, and Steve made trips there twice a year, both to replenish his stock and also to buy diamonds that customers had specifically ordered. I greatly admired the customers on the Antwerp list. I couldn't help myself. It's not just that they were willing to fork out a hefty chunk of change, it's that they wanted the best. They wanted quality. Diamonds from the regular inventory would simply not do for their pieces of jewelry. And so they would meet with Steve and pick out their own winning combination of the four Cs, and Steve would bring them back the perfect stone.

I wanted to be one of these people, but I couldn't afford it. Few could. Luckily, in addition to the custom stones, Steve would also bring back stud earrings of various sizes, and so to make myself feel like a part of the Antwerp club, I splurged and bought probably the smallest pair we had. Only one tenth of a carat, they've remained one of my favorite pieces of jewelry over the years.

A trend during my time at Carlton's, although it wasn't actually jewelry, was that of the jewelry box. Wolf Designs had a line of boxes we carried, and the part of me that liked organizing things spent hours upon hours looking at each of them and trying to decide which one to get. Full of various drawers, compartments, and velvet-lined slots, you really had to match the box to the kinds of pieces you had. And they weren't cheap either, so I felt that I really had to get this one right.

I ultimately selected a black box, compact and rectangular, complete with a handle for carrying. I put my rings in the slots, and my bracelets, earrings, and necklaces went into their own compartments. The neatness of it all delighted me, and I spent more time looking at the jewelry I owned than I did wearing it. For all my planning, it shouldn't surprise anyone that I soon had more jewelry than I could fit inside the box. While on the Carlton Jewelers payroll, it's a wonder I made any money at all.

Trilliant

I'd first met Steve after moving to Taber Glen at age nine, and it didn't take long for me spot his jewelry store. This could have been due to my love of sparkly things, or it could have been due to Taber Glen only having about five retail stores period. I didn't come around often, and when I did I was usually too shy to actually speak to anyone, but Steve began offering me the keys to the jewelry cases whenever I stopped by. I cannot possibly express how exhilarating this was. That Steve had such trust in me and also recognized how much I loved being there made me feel privileged, important, and almost grown-up. And so I would take the keys, carefully open up the cases, and briefly slip on my favorite pieces.

I've done this my whole life, such that trying on

diamonds has become a sort of needed fix for me, something I must do regularly in order to keep moving. Like refueling at a gas station, carbing up before a marathon, or periodically pulling up images of Joseph Gordon-Levitt and staring at them until I'm convinced that ending up with him is a possibility. Not that I do this.

The trouble with leaving home at age eighteen was that I would still need my jewelry fix. And without Steve around, how could I convince other jewelers throughout the country that they could trust me with the keys to their display cases? I had to resort to being a *regular customer*, subject to the boundaries of the glass that keeps gems from being out in the open. Worse, I had to *ask to try things on*, which usually meant a fair amount of this whole pretending-to-be-a-serious-customer business. Of course, my post-MBA financial situation did turn me into an actual serious customer by the time I reached my mid-twenties, but my college years provided many opportunities for some fine acting.

Not that fine acting should be required. In fact, let me be perfectly clear. I do not support any store that only services those customers who actually *look* like serious ones (i.e. are well-dressed and already clad with several custom-mounted gemstones). Further, I would like to take this opportunity to publically shame any store that does this; that refuses to take seriously those run-of-the-mill individuals who don't *appear* to be the type of people who would actually purchase fine jewelry. And my shaming extends beyond the jewelry realm. For I'll never forget how I felt one December evening while shopping at Hyphenated High-End Kitchen Store for a Christmas gift for my best friend, Ellie.

I wanted to buy Ellie a nice springform pan, as I knew she didn't have one. While it's true that it may or may not have been raining outside, I may or may not have had an umbrella, and I may or may not have chosen to put on an old, ripped-up hooded sweatshirt before racing out the door for my marathon Christmas shopping outing, that didn't mean I didn't have money to spend.

In defense of the evil saleslady to whom I'm about to refer, by the time I got to this particular outdoor shopping center and had made my way from the parking lot to the doorway of Hyphenated High-End Kitchen Store, it's quite possible that I looked alarmingly like a wet rat. Still, that's no excuse for assuming that said wet rat hadn't come into the store to purchase something. No one offered to help me, so I waded through the sea of luxury and somewhat superfluous kitchen gadgets on my own until I had picked out the nicest springform pan I could find. Ellie was a classy dame, not to mention one of my favorite people on the planet, and if anyone deserved the best, Ellie did.

When I took my item to the register and set it down on the counter, Ms. Evil looked confused. Instead of ringing it up, she just stood there looking at me as if she were waiting for something. *Oh, Lord. Had she called the police? Was my attire really that unsettling?* When she spoke, it was obvious she had taken such pause so as to craft an inflection that yielded the perfect combination of disgust and matronly condescension.

"Do you know how much this *costs?*" she asked softly, almost in a whisper.

It was the softness of her voice and its inflection that bothered me more than the actual question. The kind of hush-hush tone usually reserved for someone who's done something embarrassing and has no idea. I'd half expected her to throw a "sweetheart" on the end of her question, which she probably would have had my torn sweatshirt not been an obvious sign of filth and poverty.

I stared at Ms. Evil for several seconds, trying to craft my *own* inflection as I fought to keep myself from blurting out something like, "What's your point, bitch?" or, at the very least, "Do you think I'm *poor?*" Because what I couldn't figure out was what exactly Ms. Evil expected as a response to her question. That I would only then decide to look at the price tag, sink into a frown, and shy away from the counter and out the door? That I hadn't actually known how much the pan cost when I made the decision to purchase it? Nevertheless, I decided to take the high road and simply answer the woman's question.

"Yeah, I do."

And then I paid her, in cash, for Ellie's fancy pan, all the while shooting her a look that I hope sent the shaming message I was going for. Because treating people like they're not serious customers is simply bad business. Unless a customer causes you to fear for your own life, is physically exposing themselves, or asks if they can sleep in your back room for the night, assume they have every intention of purchasing something—whether now or in the future—until you have been proven wrong.

Even if you *have* been proven wrong, as in you've actually heard a customer say the words, "I don't have any money and won't be buying anything, I just like being around diamonds," humor them. Show them around. Invite them back. *Do it.* Do it for me. Do it for all the Joseph Gordon-Levitt fans out there who know where I'm coming from when I say there are just some things in this world we cannot go too long without.

Pear (Tear)

As a person preoccupied with a love of jewelry, the question I'm most often asked is what kind of wedding ring I want. None of my boyfriends have ever asked me this question, mind you, but for friends and family who know of my affection for all things sparkly, their assumption is that my ideas for a dream ring are as specific as they are ostentatious.

True, I've gone through phases, the earliest and longest of which was a two-carat-or-bust phase, but my philosophy on wedding rings has become remarkably similar to my philosophy on men, in that you can't select your ideal via a list of must-haves. Because as soon as you tell yourself that you're only interested in a clean-cut, hard-working, morally-stable man, you'll fall for an unkempt, unaccomplished alcoholic. Counter-intuitive as it seems, must-haves and deal-breakers have absolutely nothing to do with the chemistry that binds us to those things we inexplicably cannot do without. I should know. I fell for an unkempt, unaccomplished alcoholic.

And so it is with wedding rings, although I didn't actually believe I would get past my two-carat-or-bust phase until I fell head over heels for a much smaller ring in our very own inventory at Carlton Jewelers. It was the most bizarre thing, because the ring itself went against every must-have I'd come up with. For starters, it was small. The center stone was an embarrassing half a carat. *Half* a carat. As in not even one. Let alone two. And it was a marquise cut, which had always been my least favorite. The shape reminded me of a football, a Dairy Queen sign, things that didn't have any place being called to mind by a piece of fine jewelry. But the sheer tip-to-tip length a marquise yields actually makes it look bigger than it is, and this was not lost on me. I must have checked the specifics a thousand times over, so sure was I that the diamond must be bigger than half a carat.

So even though I would have never chosen this ring based on its description, it was a classic example of the sum of its parts phenomenon, and to look upon it put me in a kind of trance. The marquise stone sat on a platinum band that bore baby round diamonds all down both sides. The ring had a tiny wedding band attached, another thing I generally disliked, but in this particular case, the band only improved the overall appearance of the ring.

It was certainly a very diamond-heavy presentation, which probably explains the majority of my fascination. The long center stone on top of the baby rounds created some of the most dazzling sparkle I'd ever seen. But sparkle isn't for everyone, and when my mom came into the store one day, she actually looked away from the ring, almost as if it had been too bright. I'd been anxious to show it to her and was baffled by her reaction.

"There's just so much diamond," she said, although what she probably meant was, "There's just *too* much diamond."

My poor, unfortunate mother.

It occurred to me one morning as I was setting my dream ring up in its display case that since the ring was for sale, someone could, technically speaking, buy it. This filled me with a very real sense of panic. Why I hadn't thought of this before, I'm not sure. But clearly something had to be done, for I was in love with this ring and no other.

To thwart potential buyers, I began placing my ring in the very back of its display case. To the point where it was not actually displayed at all, rather it was completely hidden from view. Each morning I did this, making sure I was the one who set up that particular case, and each evening I smiled to myself as I collected the ring from its case and put it back in the safe with the other jewelry. One day down, a couple more years to go. Of course, had I known at the time just how long I would remain single, I'd have never bothered with trying to keep it in stock. I'd have prominently displayed the ring and sold it to the first pair of doe-eyed lovebirds who walked in the door. Granted, I might have rolled my eyes at them when they weren't looking, possibly spit at their backs as they walked out the door, and most certainly cried when I'd gotten home that night and been forced to stew over not having what I wanted most—which was a killer diamond.

But we never know these things when in the moment, now do we? How our lives are going to unfold and on what kind of timeline. As far as I was concerned back then, my husband was bound to show up at any moment, and I needed my dream ring to be there waiting for him.

It lasted all summer, the ring, and even managed to remain unpurchased during the school year, such that when I returned home from college for another summer at the jewelry store, my dream ring was still there looking as sparkly as ever. Damn, it was pretty. I immediately began hiding it again, and only after returning from a short vacation did I realize that the unthinkable had occurred. The ring was gone. I thrashed around inside its case, the case next to it, all the cases in the entire store. Had it been moved to a window display during my absence? Was it being polished? It *had* to be there. Or else what was to stop me from spiraling into an irreversible depression? It had been a closeout ring, and there was no way to get another. I'd already looked into it.

When I typed the item number into the computer—from memory, yes—the sad and horrible truth was that someone had bought my ring. But who? Knowing this suddenly seemed crucial to my very existence. Not that it would change anything. What would I even do with this information? Go over there and demand the ring be returned? Ask if I could come try it on every so often? No. But much like a child who is married off, I had to know it was in good hands. I had to know that these people were quality. It turned out I didn't know who the buyers were, which was a bit unusual for such a small town. All things considered, this probably made it easier.

I was to have one last day with my ring. My hopes having been restored at seeing it sitting in the ultrasonic cleaner one morning (*Praise Jesus, they've changed their minds!*), I couldn't help but smile at the mere thought of the ring making its way back to me. And my husband. Who was probably right around the corner and about to walk in the store and enter my life. But alas, the ring was only there to be cleaned, and by close of business, the owners—a woman with acrylic nails and dyed hair and a man who'd had to finance the purchase—had come to fetch it. Odd, because I pulled it out of the cleaner myself, but it just didn't have the same sparkle as it did while under my careful watch. In the back corner of the display case.

Half dutch rose

As the one whose job most closely resembled that of an intern—or insert any word that can be either loosely or directly interpreted as peon—I always ended up running store errands on slow days. Menial tasks, certainly, but I didn't mind them at all. On the contrary, I rather looked forward to these little field trips. I felt productive and useful, even if I was only being asked to walk down the street and drop something off. And more than that, I felt while out and about that I was representing the store. And this filled me with a sense of pride and privilege.

Sometimes it was as simple as lunch. Steve always ordered lunch from one of the restaurants in the few block radius that surrounded the store. Pamela and Nancy would order food as well, and a frequent task of mine became fetching their lunches. I didn't mind doing it, but I would have enjoyed it more had one of the lunches in the order been mine. As it was, I never bought my lunch. I couldn't justify it. Not when I could bring a sandwich and chips from home and save myself upwards of $10 a day.

It didn't help though that Steve made a bit of a production about where to order lunch each day. He'd seek input from others, sometimes me, and even though it was sweet for him to ask me every day if I wanted anything, it only meant that every day I had to admit once again that I couldn't afford it. Not that I ever said this, but I felt like it must have been obvious. So it's safe to say the lunch-fetching errand may have been my least favorite, because as I walked back to the store with a bag full of delicious food, I knew not only that I wasn't going to be eating any of it, but also that I would have to sit there eating my peanut butter and jelly while everyone else partook. Twenty-one years old and I hadn't made it past the school cafeteria.

Nancy sometimes sent me on errands to the drugstore down the street. It was an interesting layout for a building, one in which you walked down a bunch of stairs upon entering. Which basically meant that the store itself was underground, or at least that's how it felt. I think I'd even heard that the building had flooded once. I pictured this flood as I walked through the aisles buying things like toilet paper and Windex.

One of my favorite errands was to the shop of the engraver a few blocks away. Steve didn't do his own engraving, so whenever a customer requested it, Steve would hand it over to the engraver down the street. Or should I say, *I* would hand it over. He was a younger man than Steve, and his shop was very small. But I liked it. I *loved* it. And I've always been this way. You give me a little shop with a basic trade like engraving or cobbling and I will make every effort to patronize it. Because it's idyllic, it's charming, and I can't imagine they make any money.

I especially enjoyed this errand because everything I dropped off would eventually need to be picked up, and I loved the pickups as much as the drop-offs. Perhaps even more as I looked at the newly-etched lettering on each item. The only downside to the engraver's errand was the nagging little thought that would creep in every time I considered what this errand actually meant. Because it meant that Steve was outsourcing this partic-ular piece of his business.

Which brings me to the errand I ran most often: the post office. Let me first explain what might be the most common misconception about jewelers, and that is the word itself. It can mean so many different things, but what it probably *doesn't* mean is a person who not only knows everything about jewelry (i.e. certified gemologist) but also *does* everything jewelry (i.e. appraises, repairs, designs, and creates). The word jeweler could refer to so many different abilities and skill sets that people have come to believe that any jewelry store provides all the services they could ever need. And this is not the case.

When it came to Steve, he and his goldsmith did the more basic repairs themselves, but if ever anything was beyond their skill level or seemed particularly precarious, the items were mailed to a jewelry design center in another state. I know this because I was the one who mailed them. Nancy would assemble the job envelopes and write out detailed descriptions of and instructions for each piece, and then she'd put them all in a box, wrap the box in plain brown paper, and send me on my way with the box and some money for mailing it.

My first and immediate concern was that someone would mug me on my way to the post office. Nancy would always total the value of the pieces so I would know how much insurance to put on the package, and walking through the streets alone while holding thousands upon thousands of dollars' worth of jewelry could make even the most strong-hearted feel slightly uneasy.

But the bigger concern, the one that occupied my thoughts on the walk back to the store, was all the things that could go wrong once the package left my hands. In all the time I worked there, we never had any packages lost in the mail, but to think about how easily that could have happened put me in a bit of an internal panic. And what would we even say? *Sorry, customer, but your wedding ring was lost in the mail. These things happen.* Even though most of the repairs that came in were things like ring sizing or prong replacing and were done in house, it made me nervous to be outsourcing repairs to another facility, although this is common practice for many jewelers.

A decade after my summers at Carlton, I was living in Cleveland and would occasionally get together with the woman who had lived next door to me in Taber Glen while I was growing up. Sheri now lived in Pittsburgh, and I made the two-hour drive pretty regularly to see various friends and to absorb the delights of the city. I love Pittsburgh because it's got the same feel as Cleveland, except it's nicer and infinitely more beautiful with all those rivers and bridges. If they had an NBA team, I might have left Cleveland years ago.

While at breakfast with Sheri one day, I was filling her in on the gemology degree I was pursuing, and so the conversation turned to all things jewelry. I found it charming to hear her say that she still has Steve do all her jewelry repairs. What a testament to how much his customers love him. Living in Pennsylvania, she literally saves all her jewelry repairs for when she goes to Oregon.

"I just love that he does everything there in house," Sheri said. "That he doesn't send things out to be done by someone else."

I had oodles of post office runs that could disagree with her, but I smiled and nodded and kept eating my bacon and eggs. Because when it comes to their jewelers, maybe it's something people just need to believe. Whether or not that's true, let me offer a suggestion: If within your business there is a peon running all the errands, buy her lunch sometime. It will make her day. I promise you that.

Holland rose / double rose

I remember a project in business school that involved coming up with an idea for a new business. I was new to business as a course of study and relied heavily on my partner for the financial analysis involved, but the business idea we used was mine. Less for its merit and more for my severe lack of excitement about my partner's idea, which was something in the automotive realm.

At the time, this business idea of mine was one I would have given anything to try out; to go for. And while I've since learned that I wouldn't be the first to sell this product in this way (or even the first to use the dynamite business name I had come up with), I didn't see any reason why my idea wouldn't float me comfortably to retirement.

Until my partner determined after our careful planning that the business would generate only $45,000 per year. That would not do at all. We (he) further determined that the ideal scenario would be to open ten stores, bringing the profit up to $450,000. Now *that's* what I'm talking about. Although what I really *don't* want to talk about is how much capital it would require to open ten stores in the first place.

The age-old takeaway of the story is this: If one store makes you money, two stores could make you *more* money. So when Steve decided to expand on his Taber Glen store and open one in nearby Pinetell, it was sure to mean good things for the business, and I was happy for him. Ecstatic even. Expansion has got to be immensely satisfying for any business owner. And now Carlton Jewelers would be a chain!!

The new store immediately eclipsed the flagship store. In pretty much every way. Pinetell—still a small town but much bigger than Taber Glen—is big enough to have a downtown area of sorts. Not of the trendy or hipster variety, but a downtown with a classic, historic feel. About as charming as you can get in rural Oregon.

I'm pretty sure the space Steve rented for the new Pinetell store had been a jewelry store in the past, which probably deserves a good portion of the credit for why the Pinetell store was so effortlessly perfect almost immediately. High ceilings, dark wood paneling, and jewelry cases filled the lower floor area, and a few stairs led up to more floor space, although Steve didn't keep much up there other than his desk where he met with clients.

The back room housed a sink and fridge, a table where we all ate lunch, and the restrooms. And of course there was the workshop where Steve would sit at his bench and actually work on the jewelry. A myriad of tools and equipment sat in the workshop, but my favorites, probably because they were the only things I had the ability to operate, were the cleaning devices. The ultrasonic cleaner was the most frequently used, I guess because it was so easy to just drop things in there. It could clean a whole host of rings at once, and I enjoyed the blue color of the cleaning solution and the way the tiny vibrations would form little bubbles that would float up and away from the jewelry. It's like you could see the dirt being shaken right off.

The steamer was another favorite, as all you had to do was hit the item with some steam, dry it off, and it would sparkle like never before. You held the item with a long, metal device, a cross between tongs and tweezers, while it was being steamed to prevent yourself from getting burned. And I suppose this is the only part about operating the steamer that made me uneasy. While I never even came close to burning myself, I always worried I would. And with that loud, hissing sound each time the button was pushed, it was enough to easily unsettle anyone who was at all less than confident.

The buffer wheel wasn't exactly a cleaning device, in that it was meant more for metals than gems, but operating it was still immensely satisfying. Much like the cleaners enabled you to instantly see improved gem sparkle, the buffer had the same effect on gold. I loved seeing bands brighten several shades and their nicks and scratches removed. And all from a switch I merely had to turn on, a rapidly revolving disc I only had to brush the gold against for a few seconds.

Directly above the workshop was the only other part of the store I haven't yet mentioned. It wasn't used all the time, but it was the office where Steve's wife, Pamela, would sometimes sit while she got things done. Pamela was the business half of Carlton Jewelers, in that I have no doubt she is what kept the place running. Sure, Steve had the jewelry knowledge and skills, but Pamela is the one who paid the bills, the one who kept the inventory stocked, and the one—I'm sure—who negotiated any deals on behalf of the business.

To prevent Pamela from having to come up and down the stairs, someone had fashioned a braid, thick and made of yarn, for her to dangle out the office window. When she needed a certain check for her bookkeeping, she'd throw down the braid, we'd clip it to the end, and then she'd hoist it back up. Same thing when she had, say, a letter that needed to be mailed. She'd clip it to the end of the braid and send it out the window for me to unclip and add to the mailman's stack.

Of course, none of these inner workings were known (or would have even mattered) to the customers, as all they saw were the dazzling floor displays, the overall presentation of the fancy light fixtures glowing off of pristinely-cut gemstones. And I have yet to meet a person who has walked into Carlton Jewelers and not been so moved as to remark—whether right then or after the fact—about how beautifully striking the store is. Even though I lived in Taber Glen and Pamela frequently expressed her gratitude for having in me a floater employee who could work at either store, the only store I ever actually worked in was the one in Pinetell. And for that I couldn't have been more delighted.

The Pinetell store did so well that it was soon outperforming the Taber Glen store. Not that this should come as a surprise. It wasn't just the Pinetell store's beautiful layout and downtown corner location that gave it a sales boost, but the larger population in Pinetell also helped. There were simply more people there who could afford to buy jewelry. In fact, within a few years after I stopped working there, Carlton Jewelers had closed the Taber Glen store altogether, choosing to focus exclusively on the bigger, more profitable location in Pinetell.

Which brings me back to the topic of store expansion. Because while this was surely a sound business decision on Steve and Pamela's part, it still meant a regression of sorts. And more than that, it meant a gaping hole off of Taber Glen's Main Street. A hole that no antique shop or used book store could fill. A hole that no longer could shine the way it did every day of my childhood. And perhaps this is why it's a good thing I never went after my business school dream of opening a chain. I simply become too attached and am left unable to cut my losses. Even when they lose their sparkle.

Octagon

Sometimes it was hard not to be jealous of Steve. And I suppose it still is. Not that he isn't one of my favorite people; a man so cheerful and genuine that his effect on the customers of Taber Glen and Pinetell has always been a bit Pied Piper-esque. No, it's not his popularity that gets to me. Because I'm right there with the rest of the rats, scurrying behind him as the music plays. And I'll tell you why.

It's because Steve is the perfect blend of expertise and showman. He has the ability to sell without seeming like a salesperson, to engender trust in others, and to build community relationships that help to further elevate his brand. He's truly everything you would want in a local jeweler, a profession where trust and expertise are so key. Not only are we talking about high dollar purchases, but also ones where sentimental value (particularly on pieces customers already have) is even higher. You wouldn't leave your antique heirloom jewelry with just anyone, now would you? And of course it always meant a lot to me personally that Steve had been so kind to me over the years, and that he always remembered my love of jewelry.

When I initially approached Carlton Jewelers about working there, I went in to the Taber Glen store and nervously gave my little prepared speech to the store manager. It was disappointing that Steve wasn't around, and even more disappointing that the store manager told me she didn't think they had a hiring need at that time.

But later that same day, Steve personally called my house and told me he'd love to have me on board.

"It'll be the Pinetell store, though," he said. "And it will be minimum wage."

Who cares? I had a job. At Carlton's, which I had spent so much of my childhood admiring.

I wasn't a very good salesperson, and I certainly didn't know much about jewelry, so my anxiety around customers and my avoidance of them whenever possible could not have escaped Steve's notice. Which is why I felt genuinely touched and encouraged when during my second summer on staff, Steve made a point of telling me how much more confident I seemed, and that my skills interacting with customers had improved dramatically.

None of this really explains the jealousy I referred to earlier, so let me get back to my original point here. It was hard not to be jealous of Steve when it came to his career. He was a jeweler, the lucky son of a gun. And the way he came to own his store made me particularly envious. Because, if you want to know the truth, Steve wasn't even a Carlton.

His sister's husband, owner of Carlton Jewelers, approached him with the initial proposition. I'm not sure about the details of how this went down or what the timeline was, but Mr. Carlton introduced Steve to the idea of taking over his store.

I know this change of ownership involved Steve paying a nice chunk of change, which makes him not so unlike me and what I would have to do to obtain a store, but what I'm jealous of is that he had such a connection in the first place. Such a sure thing, such an opportunity.

It certainly must have made things easier for Steve that he didn't have to go looking for a store to buy, but the real advantage of this whole arrangement was that I bet he spent at least some amount of time under the tutelage of Mr. Carlton. Grading stones, sizing rings, working the showroom floor. By the time Steve took over ownership of the store, he probably already knew the ins and outs of running that business. Or at the very least had easy access to an expert whom he could consult and ask for help. That is the value of apprenticeship and the reason why I'm jealous that I didn't pursue jewelry from the start or get myself set up to learn from a master jeweler somewhere. Because no amount of studying can prepare you for something quite like apprenticeship can.

Take studying a foreign language. In college I took every single German class they had, studied every single textbook I could find. I learned more than most people ever do about the tenses and conjugations of the German language—I probably learned everything a person can be taught on the subject—yet even after all that book learning, I struggled to actually converse in German.

Which I guess is the point I'm trying to make. Just as a person who studies German will never learn it unless he actually goes to Germany and is forced to speak it for a good length of time, neither will a gemologist really have the ability to grade stones unless she has actually had the chance to see and analyze tons of them already. Translation: It's hard to study your way into a jewelry career, although, lucky me, it's the only option I've got.

I don't fault my dad for not becoming a jeweler, but I'd be lying if I said I didn't sometimes (read: all the time) wish he had been one. I've had many people over the course of my life express surprise over my lack of interest in following in the profession he *did* choose. This would have given me the ease of business inheritance that I seem to so covet, but I never had any desire to become a veterinarian. Not because I don't love animals, but because I love them far too much.

Considering that Steve does have children, I've always been surprised that neither of them have had any interest in taking over Carlton's. Given my own aversion to pursuing a career in veterinary medicine despite how convenient that would be, I suppose I can't blame them. Still, what I wouldn't give to have such a connection.

Heart

There's something to be said for a job that requires the use of a parking meter. There's something to be said for parking meters in general. Anything coin-operated, really. In this digital age, how refreshing. Of course, back in my Carlton Jewelers days, things were not nearly as automated as they are now, so it wasn't the coin and crank mechanism that had me so enchanted. Rather it was the adultness it engendered within me. A real job. That I had to dress up for. And park on the street for. And keep an ashtray full of quarters in my car for.

Pinetell's little downtown area only consisted of a

few blocks, and if you drove to the outskirts, two things would happen. First, you'd literally run out of road. When I think of the street I used to park on, I remember it being a dead end and running into a hillside. Second, you'd run into a hillside. The street with the parking meters was itself a hill, and a pretty steep one at that. Every morning I'd turn up the street and three-point-turn my way around so I could pull into one of the spaces facing downward.

The paved area directly behind the Carlton store had been converted into a parking lot, and Steve leased two spaces. This meant that Steve—or Pamela if Steve was at the Taber Glen store—and Nancy used them. The other person working—there were never more than three—had to hike in from the meter street. Not that I minded in the least. I didn't. Like I said, the meters were almost a perk for me. The only thing I ever worried about was what I would do if all the spaces were taken. There weren't really that many, and I lived in fear about what would happen on the morning I showed up and had nowhere to park.

Because here's the thing you have to know about me: Parking is a big deal. It always has been. I have been known to base the friends I visit and the stores I patronize based on how plentiful—and how easy to access—the parking is. It's not because I'm a parking snob. It's because I have no ability to maneuver a car in any way other than standard driving. Parallel parking on a busy city street?

Forget it. Driving somewhere I've never been and not looking the parking situation up beforehand and making sure it's one I can handle? Won't do it.

It's so bad that when my go-to garage is full or my parking plan for some reason does not work out, I seem to lack the ability to formulate a plan B. Or, I don't know, *find another garage.* My mind goes blank, I become panicky, and I end up parking much further away from my destination than necessary, just so I can find a place that doesn't require any street smarts or maneuvering skills.

Just to illustrate the severity of this handicap, let me share an example. I had a friend who worked as an RA in one of the dorms at Case Western Reserve University. I was picking her up one night, and even though she'd given me basic instructions, I was uneasy about it. I hadn't been in Cleveland all that long and I had spent exactly zero time hanging around the Case campus. When she told me to turn into the driveway area of the dorm and that there would be a pathway of sorts to get to a parking place where I could idle while I waited for her to come out, I was skeptical that her instructions would actually do the trick. Not because they weren't sufficient, but because I am so challenged behind the wheel.

I found the dorm but saw no pathway leading to a parking area. I didn't see a driveway or anything resembling one, but after inspecting the area carefully, I did notice a car-length dip in the curb. This was the only thing that could lead anywhere other than the small circle of pavement that I was currently driving laps around, so I drove onto what did actually turn out to look very much like a pathway once I got on it.

Off in search of the parking area, I wound my way slowly along the pathway, which seemed awfully narrow and winding for a road of any kind. It also seemed like a very strange place for an automobile pathway in the first place. It was almost like I was driving through the middle of campus. Which is the moment I realized that I was driving through the middle of campus.

That's right, people. The narrow width of the pathway is because it was meant for students walking, and this probably explained why so many of them were giving me strange looks as I drove around the pretty campus grounds.

At first I thought I couldn't have done it. I couldn't have actually let myself drive through the middle of a campus quad. And I had been driving for a while, so the thought that quickened my bowels was how on earth I was going to get out of this mess. I was now so far away from the curb dip that backing up through the winding path was impossible. But what if I continued and the path spit me out somewhere that wasn't big enough to accommodate a Honda Accord?

All I could do was keep going and hope to high heaven that my friend wasn't watching me from her dorm window or, more to the point, that a policeman wasn't watching from *anywhere*. Luckily, I did finally come to the sidewalk's end, and, after barely fitting between two cement posts, make it back onto the road. The real road. For cars.

I'm convinced no one else in the same situation would have done what I did; would have in panic and confusion actually assumed that the winding sidewalk cutting through campus was really the way to a parking area. And while this behind-the-wheel moment might be my all time Stupidest, know that it was not without competition, winning out over the time when I:

1. drove the wrong way on a major one-way street in downtown Cleveland.

2. went several hundred miles off track on a solo cross-country drive when the directions told me to stay on the same road for 1200 miles.

3. had to receive coaching from gas station attendants on how to not hit a pump that I had foolishly thought I possessed the skills to back up beside.

4. backed my Aunt Leah's brand new Mercedes into a big pile of metal scraps outside her husband's roofing business.

5. ditched the family car, which if you read my first book, you learned about in detail.

The point of all this is simply to illustrate how relieved I was to have metered spaces waiting for me each morning when I arrived in downtown Pinetell and to know that I wouldn't have to idiotically flounder about in the streets with no idea where to go.

On the rare day when Steve and Pamela were both at the Pinetell store and had driven separately, Nancy would be out her usual parking space in the lot behind the store. I have no reason to believe that this bothered her in any way, but she struck me as the sort of person who wasn't used to parking on the street like the hired help. It seemed as if she was embarrassed, or perhaps I was just embarrassed for her. I used to look away as she dug for the quarters she didn't usually need and filled the meter. As if not acknowledging her until we both got to the street corner could fool her into thinking I honestly had no idea how she'd gotten there. For all I knew, she'd just appeared.

As for me, I was delighted to park on the street, even if it meant I was living the life of a peon. Like I said, I loved the quarters. I *lived* for the quarters. I felt like a regular, grown-up contributor to society, and every evening as I walked back up the street, there was the initial surprise that my car was still there (Hello, Captain Paranoid. Welcome.). But then there was the glorious feeling of contentment at having worked another day, earned another dollar, and sold another diamond. Or at least having watched Nancy sell one. Ah, the life of a peon. Would you believe me if I told you that I miss it? There are quarters in my ashtray to prove it.

a word about diamonds

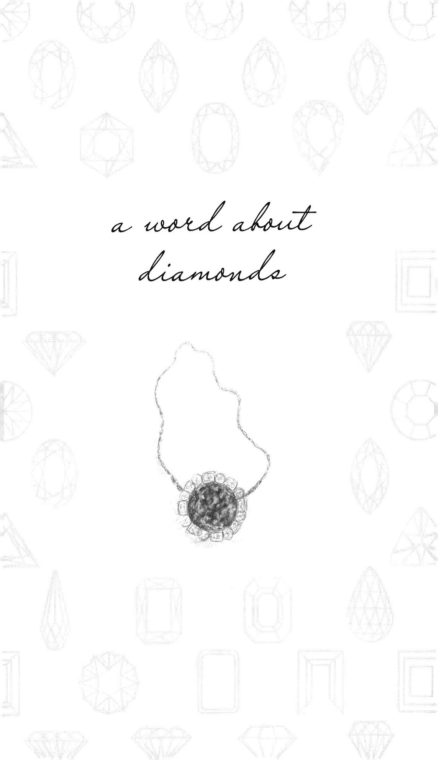

MY EARLIEST EXPOSURE TO JEWELRY PROB-ably came through the concept of birthstones. I can remember coming across a display of cheap birthstone keychains as a child and being very interested in the chart that explained which stone went with each month. It wasn't just realizing that my own birthstone was a good one, it was realizing that it was so much better than all the rest. I began taking unusual pride in my birth month, such that my birthstone became as much of an identifying factor to me as my name or gender. I was a diamond girl, and now I knew why. I had clearly been cosmically destined to be conceived at such a time in the year that would allow me to be born in April.

As to the keychains, the ones I saw in the cheap road-side market display, they were rectangles with glittery backgrounds, and they sparkled more than anything I'd ever seen up to that point. The name of the month was written in red lettering in the top right corner of each keychain, and the corresponding birthstone, synthetic of course, was embedded into the bottom left. When I saw the April keychain, I knew I had to have it. For I now knew the truth about my privileged birth month, and surely I deserved some small memento to remind me of this on a daily basis.

The trouble with the keychain was that my parents were rational people. They never spoiled me, nor were they prone to giving in to my frequent requests for useless things. If what I wanted was junk, they would attempt to reason with me until I no longer wanted it. Only it never worked that way. Because I'm sure you know as well as I do that if a child wants something, he will still want it no matter how useless it is revealed to be, and nothing about my parents' argument had made the keychain less sparkly, the zirconia stone less brilliant, or my pride at having been born in April less swollen.

I'm happy to report that I did end up with the keychain. I know this because I still have it today, although the stone has fallen out and the gold chain from which the rectangle hangs isn't as shiny as it used to be. What I'm not sure about is how exactly I came to own it, although I can tell you that it happened in one of the following two ways. I sold my soul (or at least the next several months' worth of any potential treats and presents) to my parents and they bought it for me after they realized I was never going to shut up about my right as an April girl to own such a keychain. Or I bought it with my own money, which since I didn't have any, meant that I saved for some length of time and then returned to buy it. The latter would perhaps be a more fulfilling tale, that of working for what you want, however idiotic the item, but the former is probably more likely what happened. Either way, the word was out on the concept of birthstones, and I suppose I've been a bit of a birthstone snob ever since.

What I mean is that I've never been a fan of colored stones. Not just because I was born in April, but because the deep saturation of the reds and greens and blues found in colored stones can't compare to the brilliance and fire seen in a diamond. It wasn't until I actually began studying colored stones while pursuing my gemology degree that they began to grow on me. The colors. And while diamonds will always be the epitome of gemstone beauty, I suppose the next most acceptable birthstone is the ruby of July. Ruby is the only colored stone present in any of my own personal jewelry, and its dark hue isn't too colorful to be an all-purpose stone. I might lump the hue of January's garnet into the same dark red bucket as ruby, although admittedly, garnets are not quite as stunning.

Sapphire and emerald are also somewhat all-purpose, and, along with ruby, are likely to be owned by people not even born during those months, September and

May, respectively. I prefer the deep blue of sapphire to emerald's vibrant green, but sapphire itself has become somewhat slippery in recent years, as it can come in many different colors. Sort of like a birthstone lottery for those born in September. Don't like blue? No problem. How about pink, orange, yellow, green, or purple? Take your pick. Those born in November hit a similar lottery with the recent popularity of blue topaz saving them from a lifetime with the traditional brown.

Light blue in general is a pretty color for a stone, and I'm particularly fond of March's aquamarine, as its blue is the lightest possible shade. And clarity-wise, aquamarines are clean as a whistle. To look into a good-sized aquamarine is to feel like you're inside it. That's how accessible they are. The hue of blue zircon, December's birthstone, strikes me as more artificial than that of aquamarine, and the unmistakable light purple of amethyst, the February birthstone, makes it relatively impractical for everyday jewelry. A purple stone just can't blend with things the way that violet and blue stones can, and they can end up looking tacky.

Moonstone and opal, the birthstones for June and October, are certainly impressive, although neither is typically faceted. While they each have unique beauties of their own, I find that jewelry looks best when faceted. Cabochons, the round tops you see on unfaceted stones, certainly showcase play-of-color nicely, but cabochons are a bit like the second string when it comes to fine jewelry.

Of course, there's a clear loser when it comes to birthstones, and people born in August get the ultimate shaft. Because peridot only comes in one color, and its greenish yellow to yellowish green is among the worst in the gemstone hue spectrum. In my time at Carlton Jewelers, only one person ever came looking for it. An older woman, she wasn't prepared for what she'd find when she approached me at the counter looking for a gift for her teenaged granddaughter. Part of the problem is that peridot is just terrible regardless, but the other part was that we only carried four peridot pieces.

All four were rings, and as I took the panel out of its case, I could see the excitement fade from the woman's eyes. All four rings were set in yellow gold and featured trillion-shaped stones. (Trillions are brilliants that are cut into a triangle shape.) Each of the four peridot stones in these rings were decently sized, which, in this case, only added to the woman's alarm. It's one thing for a teenager to sport an ugly stone if the piece is small and understated, but what human in their right mind wants any part of an ugly stone that's *big*; a stone that makes people think you bought it on purpose, or, worse, that you *like* it?

"Well, I guess that one's the best," the woman said after a minute as she pointed to the least offensive ring in the panel.

It may have been the only time I was literally unable to come up with any reassuring comments for a customer. I had nothing. It was, after all, my first time selling peridot, and I was as unprepared as this woman for its sheer ugliness.

When she left the store, I was overcome. Not necessarily by how badly I felt for her predicament or by how much I knew her granddaughter would hate the ring, but by how grateful I was to have a beautiful birthstone. And not just beautiful—for there are several I've mentioned here that are no strangers to beauty—but the *most* beautiful.

Sorry, colored stones, but I was a done deal long ago, and I suppose the allegiances of people like me never change.

The few. The proud. The people born in April.

Princess

The best reason I can give as to why I have such an affinity for diamonds is because they are beautiful. This needs more explanation surely, as many things in the world are beautiful. The ocean, a sunrise, pretty much anywhere in Ireland, the face of Joseph Gordon-Levitt. In the name of specificity, the thing about the beauty of diamonds that hooked me at an early age is that they sparkle. It's the sparkle that I love the best.

I'm like this with anything that sparkles, no matter how insignificant the item. Clothing, shoes, even that certain kind of cement that's got some sort of diamond powdery substance mixed in. I could spend all day on those sidewalks, walking back and forth while enjoying the play of light across all those minute reflective surfaces. But when it comes to sparkle, nothing compares to a diamond. Add to this the time and effort that goes into the cutting and fashioning of a diamond—not to mention all the conditions needed to even grow a diamond crystal in the first place—and what you get is the item that I deem more beautiful and precious than any other.

There are certainly more official terms out there than sparkle. Words like brightness, fire, and scintillation you might have heard before, and believe it or not, they each mean something different. When people talk about the brightness of a diamond, they mean how well it reflects white light. Is the stone physically bright when you look at it, or are there a lot of dark areas? Brightness is also referred to as brilliance. Fire happens when white light that's traveling through the diamond is dispersed into a rainbow of colors. And scintillation refers to the flashes of color that you see when you move a diamond back and forth. But my gemology training aside, it's all sparkle to me.

This is the main reason why, when it comes to beauty, I've never considered any colored gemstone to even be in the same ballpark as diamonds. Because the very definition of sparkle in a diamond has to do with the way those flashes of color play out. So if the stone itself is already a deep, saturated color, those flashes won't show up as well. Or at all. Which is why you don't hear terms like fire and luster when it comes to other gems. For many people, this tradeoff—fire for body color—is well worth it. I am just not one of these people.

Which is why I'm so glad that the foundation of all fine jewelry is the diamond, and that you'll see more of it than anything else when visiting a jewelry store or exhibit. It's why the diamond has its own unit in my gemology training and why the Gemological Institute of America has laboratories that are dedicated solely to the grading of diamonds. It's why diamonds are forever and why DeBeers coined that phrase in the first place. And yes, it's also why you'll find more sequence in my closet than the average person's. Because I love me some sparkle. Something about a girl's best friend.

Asscher

Perhaps this will give you an idea of the kind of extra attention we gave diamonds. Every piece of diamond jewelry we had in the store had a corresponding diamond card.

Basically a three by five index card with a small square picture of the item as well as its description and specifics (carat weight, price, etc.) written out in Pamela's handwriting. She'd fill one of these out every time we received a new piece that contained diamonds. Everything from a large diamond solitaire ring to a blue topaz necklace with a few baby diamonds lacing the sides, if it had any amount of diamond in it, then it had a diamond card.

The diamond cards were kept in a little index card filing box, the dimensions of which were hardly bigger than the index cards themselves. And when someone bought a piece with a diamond, after you rang up the transaction, boxed up the item, and sent the customer on his way, you went over to the diamond card box and fished out the item's corresponding card. You then recorded on the card who bought the item and when, and then you filed it away.

A simple and certainly manual gesture, so I have no idea why the diamond card box became my favorite part about selling a diamond, but I so loved looking through the box for the right card. I loved writing down the specifics of the purchase. The filing part of it must have appealed to the side of me that loves organization, and the recording of the details appealed to the writer in me; the part of me that saw those recordings as very official, almost like a ceremony of sorts. Something about it seemed sentimental to me, and it was all I could do not to keep myself from racing to the box every time I had cause to go there. I even volunteered to pull the cards for the transactions of other salespeople as well. And when business was slow, sometimes I would go through the entire box making sure the cards were in the right order, which was from the lowest dollar value to the highest. I loved when I found a few cards that were out of order. *How useful I am!* Dorky? Yes. Love makes fools of us all.

One of the highlights of my time at Carlton was the day when I myself made a purchase containing diamonds. It was the summer after I had graduated from college, and with an English degree but no idea how to make any money from it, I was at home working at Carlton again. Even though it had left me completely void of a life plan, I still thought I deserved something special for the accomplishment of having graduated from college, so I bought myself Antwerp diamond stud earrings. And I felt a strange sense of pride as I pulled out the box and wrote down my own name on the diamond card. Because now I was a part of it; a part of this whole diamond endeavor. Not that it's a club. But if it were, I'd be a member.

Speaking of Antwerp, it's worth mentioning that another way diamonds were given preferential treatment in the store were the twice-a-year trips Steve took to Antwerp that I've mentioned previously. Sure, he picked a few out for his own inventory to have on hand, but he also went overseas specifically looking for diamonds with the characteristics various clients had spelled out. Throughout the six months between trips, Steve would compile a list of diamonds to buy. These were not usually for the couples looking to get engaged, because couples like that rarely had the money to be shopping for custom Antwerp diamonds. Usually these Antwerp elite were older, established couples with money to burn.

As the Antwerp trips got closer, or if Steve's list was particularly light, the store would sometimes send out fliers advertising the Antwerp trip to clients who might be interested in potentially buying a diamond. I remember stamping hundreds of fluorescent-colored fliers one summer, each with a client address pre-printed. In the case of that mailing, Pamela had pulled a list of everyone who had spent a certain dollar value in the store that year. My own father showed up on the list, and while I knew he wouldn't be contacting Steve with a custom order, it made me smile to think of him as passing the threshold that had been set for people who could potentially have the buying power to make such a purchase.

If you're wondering why Steve didn't make special trips to buy other types of stones, it really goes back to the reasons why diamonds get top billing in the first place. They are the most popular stone. Period. Whereas any area, even a small timber town, has people getting married, buying anniversary bands, and upgrading their diamonds, it'd take you a lot longer than six months to come up with a list from this same small timber town of people interested in custom rubies, sapphires, and emeralds in substantial sizes. Which is why Steve focused almost exclusively on Antwerp. And I didn't mind at all. It just meant more diamond cards.

Zircon

If you've ever wondered what a diamond grading laboratory is like, it's a lot like prison. And I mean that pretty literally.

From the moment you walk into the lab you are assigned an armed police escort, and just moving from room to room requires the rat-trap technique of getting everyone inside a tiny transition cell, shutting the door to the room from which you've just come, waiting for a series of lights to blink, then opening the door to the room into which you are headed and filing out. All while under the careful watch of the police escort.

I assure you that having a big, muscular, non-smiling, armed man sizing you up for jewelry theft potential is every bit as intimidating as it sounds. There were times on the tour when I was tempted to fall out of step with the others, linger a moment longer at a certain station or machine, or poke my head around a different corner out of nothing more than innocent curiosity. But my mind would flash forward to my inevitable arrest when the security guard interpreted this innocent curiosity as a desire to stuff my pockets full of diamonds and abscond with them.

Also worth mentioning is the claustrophobia-inducing aspect of the lab as a whole. And I'm not just talking about the transition cells into which we had to be locked before being let out. I'm talking about the whole setup. Part of this was undoubtedly because this particular lab, a Gemological Institute of America diamond-grading lab, was in New York City where there is no space period. So it's no wonder that this office on Fifth Avenue was not exactly sprawling.

The interesting thing about grading diamonds is that there is, as one would expect, a huge emphasis on consistency. This lab is so prestigious and these graders are exposed to so many different diamonds that consumers need to be able to have confidence that the information listed on a diamond grading report is correct; that their stone wouldn't be given a different rating by a different grader simply because he was sitting at a different station or working under a different light source.

What I'm getting at is that the degree of consistency required in diamond grading necessitates certain mandated conditions throughout the lab. So the lighting throughout the whole office is the same, the color of the paint on all the walls is the same, and every effort is made to not vary the environments of the individual graders in any way. If cheery paint and lots of natural light were what was mandated, this might be a rocking job, but unfortunately for the graders, the lighting is kept very dim, there are absolutely no windows, and the walls are all painted gray. It is, in short, about the most depressing work environment you will ever come across in your entire life. I even brought this up to the man guiding us on the tour, and he admitted that it does cause some issues for them, namely a high amount of turnover and a lot of employees who struggle with depression. And you thought *your* office was bad.

It's a funny juxtaposition really, because what a dreary state of affairs for something as beautiful and shiny as diamonds. I was torn on my overall opinion of the lab, because while I confess to feeling what I can only describe as extreme carsickness by the time I left, I was also in a dopey state of contentment over simply being in the presence of all those diamonds. And it wasn't just the diamonds, it was the graders. I loved getting to momentarily look over their shoulders as they graded the color of a diamond by comparing it to the set of master stones sitting underneath a small fluorescent bulb. The master stones were my favorite. And every grader had their own set; a perfectly assembled spectrum of diamonds ranging from colorless to yellow to brown. What I wouldn't give for my own set of master stones. I'd compare *everything* to them, even if it had nothing to do with jewelry. What outfit should I wear today? Let's consult the master stones. Are these shoes black or blue? I bet the master stones could tell us. Is this man worth dating? Who knows, but let's go look at the master stones.

To say I had master stone envy would be an understatement, and it was the graders I kept coming back to every time we passed a new room and saw the sea of workers hunched over their stations and holding tweezer-clamped diamonds up to fluorescent bulbs. If it were me in their shoes and a group of wanna-be jewelers was passing through, I'd probably feel pretty bad-ass. *I know stuff*, is what I'd think to myself every time outsiders walked by. *I get to play with diamonds all day.* And maybe that *is* what they think to themselves. Maybe they have to in order to fight off the crippling depression that would hit them otherwise.

I would have loved to ask one of them, but the police escort was looking at me. And I didn't want to be shot down. Or frisked. Or put on some sort of "bad list" in the industry. So I kept my mouth shut and got back into the rat trap and was eventually spit back out onto busy Fifth Avenue where even the overwhelming amount of cigarette smoke was a welcome change to the dimly-lit cells and drab-colored clothing. I can't believe I'm saying this, but as much as I love diamonds, that's one job I just don't think I could do.

But I'd still like my own master stones.

Sphere

While at a recent work event, my entire department ended up stranded at Cleveland's Whirlyball facility. As a side note, if you haven't played Whirlyball, it's worth looking into. Trust me. With time to kill and no means of transporting our large group, people had no choice but to sit around and continue taking advantage of the open bar. The open bar on the company's dime. As a non-drinker, being the only one who's not drinking is something I'm used to, although it never gets any easier to endure. The way it smells, the way people act, the overwhelming there's-nowhere-I'd-want-to-be-less-right-now feeling.

This Whirlyball afternoon was particularly torturous, as I had not anticipated the downtime of being stranded. If only I had brought a book, a computer, an old term paper to edit, a lanyard to tie, anything. And I did not at the time have a Smart phone either, so I did what any sensible girl would do to stave off twiddling her thumbs. I asked all the women, including my boss, to hand over their wedding rings.

I'd seen them all before and never ceased to be amazed at how impressive these girls' diamonds were.

My boss had a large marquise, which isn't a shape you see very often these days. The jacket that encased the diamond seemed massive for having to surround such a long center stone, and the overall impression the ring left was, well, impressive.

One girl had a round diamond that was bezel set, and the ring was soldered to a diamond wedding band. And she had a diamond anniversary band that I particularly loved.

Another girl had a smallish round diamond surrounded by a sparkling (if not somewhat overwhelming) sea of small, almost pave-style diamonds. The little diamonds were everywhere. In rows around the band, up the sides. The ring almost glowed.

But my favorite in the bunch was the good-sized round stone belonging to the girl who sat in the cube across from me. The setting, white gold with touches of yellow, was similar to many I'd seen on other girls and consequently didn't have the unique factor as did the other three I've described, but the diamond, which had belonged to her grandmother, was truly spectacular. No obvious inclusions to be seen with the naked eye, and just a bright, pure look to the whole stone.

After lining all the rings up on the table in front of me, I took turns trying them on, rotating them back and forth, asking an occasional question of their owners. It's the sort of thing I could do for hours, and for some reason it got me thinking about the collective carat weight of our entire office building. These were not the only women with some serious rocks on their hands. And it was at that moment, borne out of sheer, stranded boredom, that I had the sudden urge to share a secret I'd been harboring.

"I think I know something about a woman in our building," I offered.

And I'm not sure if it was the alcohol in their systems or the X chromosomes in their genetic makeups, but my co-workers ate it right up. Their eyes widened and they leaned in, their faces close together. They could have been children on Christmas morning. Even our department director, a man, was listening in spite of himself. They were ready for something good.

"I think someone in our building has a fake diamond in her wedding ring."

My boss and the girl with the bezel set ring quickly turned and looked at each other, as if trying to read the other person's mind.

"It's got to be Tracy," they offered first to each other, then to me as they repeated the name.

Tracy was a director who worked on another floor, and I had never so much as seen her ring. I said as much and then spilled my secret.

"Lola Montgomery."

Lola was also a director, and I'd studied her ring quite a bit. She even tried to hire me once, and as I sat across the table listening to her try to sell me on a position I didn't want and ultimately didn't take, I was distracted by her ring.

The stone was huge and hard to miss as she waved her arms and gestured emphatically throughout the discussion. That something was wrong with the diamond was obvious right away. It looked hollow, lacked depth, and for a girl who has seen a lot of diamonds, it simply seemed different. Every time I've ended up in Lola's company, I've studied the ring as best I could and come to the same conclusion. And this is positively baffling. Because what would have to be true in order for a woman to be walking around with a fake diamond? The chart below is the best I can figure.

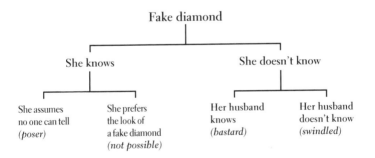

The most surprising to me is the leftmost branch of the above diagram—when a woman knows her huge diamond is fake and for some reason still wants us to believe she's the kind of person who owns a huge diamond. This kind of woman assumes the people she comes into contact with don't know enough about gemstones to call her bluff, and while this is true in the vast majority of cases, it's not a foolproof bet. It's like Latinas having a conversation in front of a white girl in which they are talking about how unfortunately skinny and pale she is. It's all fun and games until the flaca and palida chica suddenly reveals in dramatic fashion that she can speak Spanish. Booyah. *Translate that, bitches.*

Turning our attention to the She Doesn't Know section of the bracket, this is certainly a more forgiving reason for a woman to have a fake diamond. In the case of both the Swindled and Bastard branches, she's a victim. And let's explore this for a minute, because these things do happen.

First of all, it's amazing the amount of trust a woman must have to accept a diamond when she more often than not has no idea where it came from. Clearly the more weighty element in such a situation would be the amount of trust a woman must have to accept a marriage proposal and forever join her life with someone else's, but for now, let's table this and focus on the diamond. I'm not talking about the uncertainty this woman has about what country or which mine the diamond came from. I'm talking about the way her prospective spouse obtained the ring. Who did he buy it from? Is this person or establishment trustworthy? How much does he really know about the diamond he bought?

Admittedly, this is not nearly as relevant as it once was, as women now are so often involved with the selection of the ring—even accompanying their men to pick it out. And maybe I'm not giving the trust women have in their men enough credit. I mean, if the man you love presents you with a diamond ring, there's no reason you should believe it's anything less than genuine and of good quality. But the point I'm trying to make is that people do get swindled. Remember the classic *Everybody Loves Raymond* episode where he spends a small fortune to replace his wife's lost ring only to learn that the original ring he'd been sold was a fake? Don't let the TV show fakeness or Raymond's stupidity lull you into a false sense of security, because plenty of golden-hearted men get conned in the jewelry business; this is something we'll never be able to totally eliminate as long as agency and greed exist in this world.

In many ways, the odds of getting gemologically hoodwinked have dramatically decreased. The industry is riddled with various codes and commitments to ethical standards, and as a sue-happy society, you'd have a hard time fighting a case if someone could prove you'd sold them a fake. But in other ways, the situation has gotten worse due to the increased sophistication of simulant gemstone production. While at a jewelry workshop recently, the presenter told of a new "hybrid" ruby—composed predominantly of glass—that's been particularly difficult to separate from the real thing.

So what chance does a gem-clueless man have against such trickery? What chance does his bride have of ever knowing the truth about her diamond? To be clear, the She Doesn't Know section of the bracket is the only acceptable one. In Lola's case, it's the only way I can look her in the eye the next time we're sitting at the same conference room table.

Back to my big reveal in the Whirlyball lobby—it didn't pack quite the punch I'd anticipated, as my co-workers weren't very familiar with Lola or her ring, but still, the thought of any woman going around sporting a fat, fake diamond is pretty juicy. *That* was unanimous. And as for this Tracy person, whoever she was, I somehow had to check out her ring. I wondered which branch of the bracket she fell into. And I wondered if she knew I spoke Spanish.

Bead

Despite its political and historical significance to this country, Washington D.C. has never appealed to me much. When planning a trip east, however brief, it's hard to pick any other city when I know that Manhattan is sitting there in all its glory. The on-foot morning commuters flooding the sidewalks, the lights and sights of Broadway filling Times Square with a hope you can almost taste, the tiny apartments that still leave you feeling like the luckiest girl in the world just to have a few square feet in such a city. Then there's the rich culture and variety of neighborhoods and foods that spring up as a result, the thin crust pizza, the endless options of things to do and places to go, the increased probability of running into a celebrity. Not to mention the flagship Tiffany store.

At some point in my late twenties, I did finally convince myself to book a trip to our nation's capital, less so because of the city and more so because a good friend whom I hadn't seen in years lived there. I told my friend, Zoey, what I wanted to do, which was basically the types of things I felt obligated to do as a tourist. And as an American. And I'm not saying I didn't enjoy myself. I'm not saying I wasn't impressed by all the monuments and museums we took in over the next couple of days. I was. Very much so. Who knew that the sculpture of the soldiers holding up the flag was so big? After seeing it in pictures my whole life, I was amazed to stare up at its greatness. The gravestones, rows upon rows of them, each a neat, white marker of seeming anonymity. The inspiring quotes etched in stone surrounding the presidential monuments. No, I'm not saying I wasn't moved, because it would be impossible to not be.

What I'm saying is that as soon as Zoey told me about a jewelry exhibit in one of the Smithsonian museums, it was all I wanted to see. Battles fought, lives lost, history shmistory. Just get me to the Smithsonian pronto.

Jewelry lover that I am, for the life of me I'm not sure how I hadn't known about the Smithsonian exhibit, and I spent the majority of my first and only Saturday afternoon in DC holed up looking at the individual pieces. Some were more stunning than others, but all were beautiful and unique and incredibly ornate as only jewelry from eras past is. I took my time, pausing at each case to read about the piece, and just about my only complaint was the sheer volume of people doing the exact same thing. Man, was it crowded. I knew why *I* was there, but why were so many others? Why weren't they out shading names of ancestors onto sheets of paper, dabbing tears at Arlington, paying tribute to the founding fathers? *What was wrong with people??*

I fought the crowds and made my way through the exhibit, which culminates in a room bearing a single rotating glass case. A very large case. And what I for some inexplicable reason hadn't realized until reaching the end of the exhibit that day in the Smithsonian was the contents of that final case. Because suddenly I was face to face with the Hope Diamond. The freaking Hope Diamond, people. At over forty-five carats, it's the world's largest blue diamond. And I was looking at it.

I moved as close as I could. No small task given how the crowd was swelling in the small room. Naturally, I stared at the diamond for much longer than what was probably considerate, but I couldn't help myself. Resting on a slanted gray column and shining under a spotlight, the blue stone was magnificent. It was loose, by itself, temporarily removed from the diamond setting that typically encases it. The setting, complete with a chain also made from good-sized diamonds, was sitting at the bottom of the gray column, and just in front of the platform that held everything was a plaque giving a brief description of the setting and how long the Hope has been in it.

The Hope Diamond got its name from the family who owned it in the 1830s. Certainly the diamond had existed before then, and its somewhat treacherous past included such names as King Louis XVI and his wife, Marie Antoinette. When a Hope descendent had to sell the diamond due to financial mismanagement, it made its way through a chain of jewelry merchants, including Cartier, and was ultimately bought by Harry Winston in 1949. Winston donated it to the Smithsonian, which explains why a bust of Harry Winston is located mere feet away from the Hope Diamond today.

It didn't take long to notice—from my vantage point at the very front—that the case which housed the Hope Diamond, or at least the gray column on which it directly sat, rotated every so often. Meant to give people the room over the chance to see it up close without creating a bottleneck (and possible pandemonium) on one side, you'd hear a little electronic whir every fifteen seconds or so as the column would turn ninety degrees.

I found this annoying, but I suppose it's better than the crowd control method used in England. Tourists wanting to get a glimpse of the crown jewels are rushed passed via a moving walkway. That I would be one of the crazies walking against the grain until I'd either had my fill or been arrested goes without saying.

As it was, I stayed put in front of the Hope Diamond long enough to see it rotate the full 360 degrees. But when it rotated away for the second time, I stayed put.

Just one more time.

And then it had made its way around once more and still I didn't budge.

I've come all this way. I might as well get another glimpse.

It came around again.

It's just so pretty.

And again.

You can't make me leave.

And then I left, but not before getting my picture taken next to Harry Winston's bust and buying a coffee mug bearing a close-up shot of the stone. Which I still use every day at the office, by the way, and which is still frequently mistaken for Kate Middleton's sapphire. *As if.*

I've asked myself many times what this story says about me; that I was more interested in seeing the Hope Diamond than the historical monuments dedicated to the establishment of this great nation. I've concluded that it's not for a lack of patriotism, because I felt an enormous amount of gratitude and awe while in D.C. For the men who had such vision centuries ago, for the people who have given their lives over the course of this country's existence in defense of it, for the freedoms we enjoy as Americans.

See, even as I am writing these words, my eyes are spilling over, and that's just it. I am a person who is not particularly moved by these monuments, because I am moved by what they represent every day. I don't need to be there to appreciate them. All I need to do is vote in every election, practice religion as I see fit, and fall asleep feeling safe in my bed to be reminded of those who championed this country into being and feel over-whelmingly confused as to why I've been blessed enough to live here.

Diamonds will always command my attention when they're in front of me, and that's something I can't help. They are arrestingly beautiful, and I'm not around anything as magnificent as the Hope very often. So when I am, I take advantage. But aside from the occasional story of a legendary jewel with an intriguing past, beauty is just about all that jewels hold for me. For all of us. So lest anyone get the impression that my priorities are out of whack, here is the bottom line: I love diamonds, but they've never brought me to tears over how lucky I am.

God bless Washington D.C. God bless America.

I just don't see why God can't also bless Harry Winston.

the family jewels

MY MOM SAW WHITE GOLD COMING DECADES before it actually did. She was *so* ahead of the curve. In actuality, Mom's wedding ring metal of choice had nothing to do with appearances or being trendy, because she was never particularly concerned with either. Or maybe it's that she's always preferred to spend her money on other things. Like braces for her children. For which, by the way, I will forever be grateful. Not just for the braces, but for a mother who was such a shining example of selflessness and sacrifice.

So it wasn't out of a desire to be trendy or different that Mom went with white gold. It was simply because she liked it better. Which was unusual for 1978. It would have been unusual for any bride in the latter half of the twentieth century. I'll never understand why yellow gold was so popular for so many years, but preferring the silver look myself, I've always taken a strange amount of pride in knowing that my mom's wedding ring is white gold.

She and my dad were in college and pretty close to penniless, so it goes without saying that her ring isn't anything grand. Opting to go for the biggest diamond they could afford even if it meant slightly lower clarity, it still can't be any bigger than half a carat, although I've never actually asked. The way it sits up high in the head and is soldered to a thin wedding band has always made it seem substantial enough to me. I love that it's a solitaire ring, because I've seen relatively few people over the course of my life whose rings do not contain any amount of additional diamonds or embellishments.

It's rare for Mom to not be wearing her ring, but I would occasionally see it sitting on her bathroom counter. At some point during my childhood, I took it upon myself to provide her with a box to keep it in. Nevermind that the ring wouldn't even need the box very often, but Mom acted like she'd been handed nothing short of the world when I presented her with a tiny, daisy-covered circular box in which she could keep her ring when it wasn't being worn. Thinking about it now, it reminds me of that Billy Collins poem about presenting his mother with the lanyard he'd made at camp, and how despite her gifts to him of life, limb, and love, he thought the lanyard would be enough to make them even. Maybe I wouldn't go quite that far with the ring box, but it is true that as a child you can feel yourself being transformed into a hero in moments like these. *Look at how happy she is. It is exactly what she would have chosen if everything in the world were right in front of her. She will cherish it forever. I am the absolute best gift giver.*

Despite having the box, which, admittedly, was a bit cumbersome and not even meant to be used for a ring, the place Mom most often left her ring was on the sill of the window at the kitchen sink. There was a small gold bell that she kept on that sill, sometimes she'd ring it when dinner was ready, and whenever she was washing dishes or mixing meatloaf by hand she'd take off her ring and put it on the handle of the bell. It would slide down and rest lopsided on top of the bell itself, and I can remember seeing it there sometimes when I went to the sink to wash up. Even though it meant she wasn't keeping it in the daisy box, I would find myself smiling at the ring's makeshift home. And while I might then have turned right around and complained incessantly through dinner about the injustice of having to eat her homemade lentil soup, that doesn't mean I didn't end up back at that windowsill later on in the evening. Inevitably I'd slip the ring off the bell handle, place it on my own finger, and hope it would turn me into a woman as wonderful as my mother.

In a society where it's quite common for women who have been married for long periods of time to have upgraded to better, more expensive rings, I love that my own mother's ring is still the same as it was back in 1978. At family gatherings over the years, I've noticed that a few of her sisters have upgraded and now sport bigger diamonds. Not to mention, they've ditched their yellow gold in favor of white. (Told you my mom was ahead of the curve.)

Maybe this is just the natural course of things once a couple is a few decades into their marriage and financially able to buy a ring they never could have afforded at the time of the proposal. But there's something about sticking with one's original ring that resonates with the writer in me, the romantic. Unless you've secretly always hated the ring your husband picked out, and maybe even if you have, I think you ought to stick with it. For better or for worse. For white or for yellow.

Trap

I suppose there's not as much to say about my dad's wedding ring. This is less a reflection on my dad as it is a reflection on men's jewelry in general. There's just not much of it. Which, if you ask me, is exactly how it should be. If you are a man and you wear jewelry, please resolve to stop. Stop it right now. Whether an earring, a hemp necklace, a gold chain, a ring other than your wedding ring, or a pair of custom cuff-links, just stop all of it. And this coming from a jewelry lover.

I know, I know, it's so contradictory of me. And a little judgey-wudgey. Perhaps it's because things like ruggedness and scruff are what I appreciate most in a man, so a gesture as dramatic and calculated as draping a chain around your neck or affixing something shiny to the ends of your sleeves doesn't do much to contribute to the "man equals cowboy" illusion I've got going in my mind.

Wedding rings are really the only jewelry space in which men play, and while this is certainly a significant source of business for jewelers, it's not one about which I have many opinions. In fact, my thoughts on men's wedding rings can be summed up in three succinct and completely unrelated bullets.

First, let's talk about diamonds. When it comes to a man's wedding ring, to diamond or not to diamond really shouldn't be the question. And for most men, luckily, it isn't. Personally, I have mixed feelings on the subject. On one hand, I'm obsessed with diamonds. There is nothing more beautiful to me, and sometimes when I see a man with a channel-set row of small diamonds in his ring, it impresses me. It's almost powerful. I mean, here's a man who wanted diamonds in his ring and doesn't care a snit about them being a woman's gem. Er, along with all the others. But inevitably, the admiration I feel for his not-so-ballsy-and-consequently-very-ballsy decision to bling out his wedding ring will give way to sheer judgment. Because, come on. *Diamonds?* Really, men? Ultimately I'm just not sure I can support it.

Second, let's switch to metals, which is the more meaty subject when it comes to men's rings. Surely white and yellow gold have always been king, but with newcomers such as tungsten and titanium in recent years, there's more to the decision than simply color. Titanium is particularly sexy, and I love the gray color and unique look. You can easily look into a case and identify the titanium rings for their gray, matte appearance, and the lightness of titanium is nothing short of delightful. It seems to defy all principles of science that solid matter, a metal, should be so light. Although for all the praise I'm giving it, let me caution you men out there on one particular aspect of titanium. Its chemical properties make sizing it impossible, so if you go with titanium, be prepared to never gain or lose more than a few pounds. Or else be prepared to buy a new ring with every couple of pant sizes.

Lastly, let's talk about replacing a man's ring. Because the odds of a man losing his wedding ring are very high. And the odds of a man losing his wedding ring more than once are not any lower. Why is this? Men do forget things more often than women, they aren't as enthused with jewelry to begin with, and since men's rings are of such small comparative value, there likely isn't that built-in detector that says "WHERE IS YOUR RING AT

THIS VERY MOMENT!?" like there is in the brains of women. But sometimes I wonder if this tendency of men to lose their rings isn't related to a much simpler fact: they take them off. Could this be it? Do men take off their rings more often than women?

It doesn't really make much sense, as men don't have nearly as many reasons for this as women do. Why, I can think of a dozen reasons right now as to why a woman might need to remove her ring. Think mixing meatloaf, doing dishes, putting on lotion, taking the baby to swimming lessons, etc. So men, why you gotta be taking off your rings all the time? Unless the despicable truth is you don't always want to appear married, I can't really come up with a valid reason for frequent ring removal.

It's what I've always loved most about my dad's ring—that I've never seen him not wearing it. A standard-sized white gold band, it's on his finger no matter what he's doing. Even when in surgery, he's wearing it. I know this because of all the years I used to help out at his clinic. I would watch his hands as he worked, carefully mending the organs of animals, and for some reason my eyes were always drawn to the outline of his ring under his colored plastic gloves. Whether covered in blood or delicately stitching shut an incision with scissors and suture string, it filled me with sense of satisfaction that through it all, he wore his wedding ring. Which is probably why he's never lost it. Men of the world, take note, take care, and don't take it off.

Portuguese rose

I would adore my Aunt Leah even if she didn't have a two carat wedding ring, but I might not adore her quite as much. In all seriousness, my affections cannot be swayed by the mere presence of bling, but if they could, Leah would have a definite advantage. And having access in my immediate circle to a two carat diamond was just about the biggest perk my teenage self could imagine.

Every family function found me staring at her ring, desperately wanting to try it on. As a lover of jewelry without a ring of my own, I've become an expert at asking to try on people's rings, but I try to be sensitive about when and how I do it. Sometimes when sizing up a woman's response to such a request you glean that she wouldn't necessarily be very excited (or even willing) to remove her ring and hand it over to you. So I've learned to hold back and first get a sense of how such a request would go over. And in many instances, I decide not to ask at all.

That's what was so great about Leah. Because she didn't even wait for me to ask. She just knew I'd want to try on her ring and would always remember to supply me with an opportunity to do just that. She'd pass it over to me in church, or sometimes for no reason at all she'd just plop it into my hand.

One of my favorite memories of Leah and her ring happened when all of us were waiting in a restaurant lobby to be seated. In the midst of a family gathering of sorts, we were at the Oregon coast, and it's worth noting that the Oregon coast is cold pretty much year round. So we wanted chowder. Pronto. All the cousins were sitting in a row on one of the lobby benches, and as a way to keep us entertained—and because this is just the sort of thing that aunts do—Leah began doling out quarters for us to spend on the contents of the lobby candy machines. She walked down the row plopping coins into each outstretched hand, and when she got to me, what she plopped in my hand felt much heavier than a quarter. I smiled down at the ring and reveled in how seamlessly she had done it. Quarter, quarter, quarter, quarter, quarter, ring.

Sort of like when we all play Killer Yahtzee—a round of Yahtzee in which the loser must do something unpleasant—around my grandparents' dining room table. A game as hilarious as it is competitive, at some point during each game, Leah will sneak about a dozen extra die into the cup, such that when she empties its contents on this chosen gag roll, we're all shocked and baffled at suddenly seeing so many die on the table. I can honestly say that I have never actually seen her procure the extra die or stick them in the cup. And I can just as honestly say that it has never *not* had me in complete hysterics to see all those die suddenly poured out onto the table, Leah feigning excitement at her own good fortune. "Look at all those dots!" she'll say.

Such was my delight that day in the restaurant lobby with her wedding ring unexpectedly in the palm of my hand. My cousins returned to the bench with their fistfuls of candy, but I was equally if not more content just to stare at the beautiful diamond now on my finger. The waiters could have taken as long as they wanted with our table. In a world with two carat diamonds, who even *needs* chowder?

There are a few things I've learned from my time spent bonding with Leah's ring, and one is that I have very small fingers. It's the reason why I could never really wear the ring around. My time with it was usually restricted to a sedentary activity like sitting in church. Or on a bench in a restaurant lobby. Not that Leah herself imposed these or any other restrictions, but I didn't have enough faith that the ring wouldn't fall off in the middle of some activity. Like walking across the room. Or putting my hair behind my ear. Because let me be perfectly clear. While I consider myself among the most trustworthy jewelry sitters on the planet, two carats is an awful lot to be responsible for. Especially when you can't even turn your hand upside down without them falling off.

I've also learned that two carats, along with the metal

they sit in, are very heavy, and as much as I love the thought of owning a ring just like Leah's, that's an awful lot of weight for a hand to support day in and day out. The longest I ever had it on was one afternoon while Leah was golfing. It's the only time I ever knew her to golf, but I remember riding in the golf cart thinking, "Boy, this ring is such a load." Quite a blasphemous thought for a dyed-in-the-wool jewelry lover, but life is nothing if not a lesson in tradeoffs.

For as much as I've admired it over the years, I've never actually asked Leah about the specifics of the ring, nor have we discussed them really at all. I cannot tell you for sure the carat weight (two is just a guess), color, or clarity. And I suppose in many ways it's strange that I haven't pressed Leah for all the details, but something else I've learned about jewelry over the years is that it's usually not appropriate to ask those types of questions. It can quickly turn into a judgey-wudgey fest or a pity party, neither of which are pleasant.

Not that I worry about either of those things happening with Leah, it's more that I think of her ring as some kind of glorious ideal, and something about knowing as little about it as possible helps keep it on a pedestal of sorts.

In recent years I haven't seen Leah's ring much, mostly because she's usually traveling when I see her, and much for the same reason as wearing a ring that's too big, wearing a ring while traveling significantly increases

your chance of losing track of it somehow. Leah is more
likely these days to travel with the fancy-cut garnet ring
her husband recently bought her as a birthday gift. The
same fancy-cut garnet ring that she passed down the pew
to me while we were in church this past Christmas, and
which I unfortunately forgot to take off before we headed
up to the front to perform our annual family Christmas
violin number. Try keeping a loose ring on your finger
through *that*.

Marigold

Shortly after being accepted to business school, I had a
rather profitable conversation with my sister. Kate was at
the time halfway done with her own Masters program,
and we lived in the same city. About half a block away
from each other, actually.

"There's no way you're going to finish that program
and still be single," she said.

I was intrigued. *What on earth?* I knew myself and
my luck with men, and I thought it quite likely that I
would still be single when I finished business school.

"Yes, there is," I replied.

I, in fact, could not imagine being so lucky as to find

the man of my dreams while in graduate school. Sure, it happens often enough, the age-old tale of the lovebirds who met while in college, but so far the universe hadn't given me any indication that it would be so easy for me. My dating track record had me pretty convinced it would take a lot more than two years and a hefty tuition bill to land myself a husband. I was starting to think that God would, as he had done with Eve, need to stick me on a planet where the one man alive had no other choice.

"No, you'll be married," Kate said again.

"I don't think I will be."

"Want to put some money on that?"

Her confidence surprised me, but this seemed like a win-win. I would either get a husband or get whatever amount of money she placed on the table. I was picturing fifty bucks. One hundred tops.

"I'll bet you a trip to Germany that you're married."

Eyes wide and mouth hanging open.

Done.

As it happened, the summer before I started my Masters program, she herself began dating someone. They were engaged by Thanksgiving, and her boyfriend, Jeff, assigned me a small role in the proposal.

It should come as no surprise that my involvement centered around the engagement ring. I was to pick it up at the jewelry store and hand it off to Jeff the following day. And while I wasn't jealous over her getting married, I confess that walking into the store and realizing that Kate had found one of surely the few men on earth who were willing—no questions asked, no qualms about money—to spend thousands of dollars on a ring (*the* ring) just about made me fall to the floor and weep over how unfair it was that some man wasn't there right then to do the same thing for me.

Kate's ring was nothing like the one I would choose for myself, but it was impossible not to think it beautiful. I hadn't seen the ring until I picked it up, and I opened the tiny jewelry box to reveal a good-sized princess-cut diamond on a delicate white gold band. The band, probably only one millimeter thick, was embedded with tiny melee diamonds down both sides. Jeff had also arranged for a wedding band of similar thickness with alternating diamonds and rubies, but that wasn't part of my day before pickup.

If you're wondering whether I tried on my sister's ring before she got it, of course I did. I'd have been a fool not to. I'm a diamond girl, remember? Surely the thorough inspection I gave it was justified. I even took it with me to a small study group that evening, as the thought of leaving it sitting on the counter in my college-town apartment—which didn't even have so much as a deadbolt—terrified the part of me that knew my highest priority that evening was keeping the ring safe. It might have fared just fine on the counter, but I wanted to be sure. I wanted it with me. To feel the shape of the little box in my purse. To sneak peeks and verify its safety

every so often. To imagine myself as an amalgam of Jack
Bauer as I fought off all manner of evil and danger and
civilization-ending weaponized viruses, all in an effort to
protect and successfully hand off the goods the following
afternoon.

I'm not sure Jeff realized exactly who he'd entrusted
with this mission; the girl who always insisted on riding
in the same car as her luggage during a family trip—
even if the two cars had the exact same route, itinerary,
and ultimate destination goal. The girl who—speaking
of Jack Bauer—refused to place her prize Christmas
gift of the first two 24 seasons on DVD in her checked
luggage and instead carried them on her person from
airport to airport while returning from Christmas break.
Or maybe he did. Maybe this is exactly why he picked
me. If I'm this protective over a weekend's worth of
clothes and a few DVDs, imagine how much more
devoted I am to the safety of a diamond, particularly
when it belongs to someone else.

I guess the point of this story is that when it comes
to diamonds, I will guard them with my life. And being
guardian of Kate's ring, even only for one night, is something I won't ever forget. If she and I were to live in the
same city on the eve of my engagement, it's an experience I would want her to have as well. The chance to
reflect on all those years we had together, back when it
was just us, and even when it wasn't but still somehow
seemed like only me and her. The chance to think about

her sister's future as a person with a husband, a child, another life apart from the one she'd had with me. The chance to steal glances at the ring throughout the night, to know she'd been trusted with its care.

That night with Kate's ring, I may not have had a diamond of my own...or a man wanting to marry me...or a man period...but I had Kate. And the ring meant that *she* now had a man. A man who was obviously crazy about her. A man who, despite my lack of warmth toward him in the months leading up to the engagement, was trying to involve his future sister-in-law wherever he could. A man who in all respects appeared to be a keeper.

Kate still owes me that trip to Germany, so here's hoping that Jeff is also a man who won't mind at all when she leaves him with the kids in order to gallivant around Europe with her sister.

Maybe we can make a pit stop in Antwerp.

Sunflower

My brother ordered his wife's wedding ring through the mail. Quite a contrast from the pristine princess-cut sparkler that Jeff bought for my sister, this mail-order silver ring was embedded with a single baby ruby.

If this method of obtaining a ring makes you worried about my brother's relationship, would it make you feel better to know that both he and his wife were nineteen when they got married, dealt with significant emotional instability, and had no clue about life as adults? Yeah, it didn't make me feel better either. In fact, I was downright distressed to learn of my kid brother's impending nuptials. He'd only recently rebounded from a few very rough teenage years, and marriage seemed like too much too soon.

But I suppose what bothered me even more than his seemingly still-fragile state was the fact that he was seven years younger than I was. And the more my romantically unattached twenty-six-year-old self thought about it, the more I realized that never in any version of my life had I envisioned him getting married before I did. To be honest, I was sad. I was sad to be losing him to this girl I had never even met; sad that he would no longer turn to me with all his questions and problems; sad that he had passed me up in terms of major life milestones.

I remember his excitement when he told me over the phone that the ring was on the way. Between the engagement and the mail-order ring, I tried to stay calm as I did my best to match his excitement. They'd initially talked about a year-long engagement, which gave me some relief. I could totally find a man of my own to marry in a year. But they ultimately opted for a December wedding rather than waiting until the end of the following summer. All I could do was panic and hope they might break it off.

Of course, everything changed when I met her. Because she was perfect. *They* were perfect. It was the day before their wedding, and while I tried to convince him to cut his long, red hair, even then she knew better. He kept it long, and in the wedding pictures—even if he bore a striking resemblance to Ron Weasley—he looked totally at ease and himself.

The wedding was followed by a luncheon in another city, about an hour's drive, and the luncheon was followed by a reception in yet another city, which took another hour and a half to reach. Add to this the frosty conditions of winter, and it felt like I spent the entire day in the car. And since my brother and now sister-in-law's eighteen-year-old friends had flown in with no thought to transportation, I ended up shuttling them with me across the state. I didn't mind doing it, and I suppose I couldn't fault my brother for not thinking all these details through, but when these girls began talking about their own weddings as if they had no other life plans, I had a strong urge to speak up.

Because every girl thinks she'll get married young, and every girl, whether or not she will admit it, secretly *hopes* she'll get married young. I know I did. In fact, I spent a good portion of the summer I graduated from high school thinking about the shocking realization that I could theoretically be married by the following summer. How flattering to be "picked" by a suitor so soon. I pictured some college boy falling head over heels for me and us having a baby right away. I wanted to be one of those moms who was still young enough to be cool when her kids were old enough to appreciate it.

Not that being single at age twenty-six made me feel like I was old or that I had failed, but it made me wish I had spent more time in my youth acknowledging that life might not turn out quite the way I had planned. And that's what I wanted to tell these girls. To not just assume that marriage will happen when you want it to, or that it will happen at all. To live your life the way it unfolds, to take chances and learn new things and move to new cities, to not be afraid of being fabulous alone.

At the reception I started becoming a bit panicky that this was it. That my baby brother was about to drive away with his wife. That he would never again need me in the way he always had. That our relationship might change more than I could handle. When they announced a "money dance" for the bride and groom and people began putting various bills in a jar for a chance to dance with one of them, I found myself hesitating. Because I knew I would cry. And I didn't want to be responsible for turning into a weepy mess and ruining the night. But I really wanted to dance with my brother at his wedding.

Sitting next to a good friend of mine who had come to the reception in order to see me, I confessed to her that a fear of crying was the reason why I was being a wallflower in that particular moment. I knew I would regret not dancing with my brother, but I probably still wouldn't have left my seat had my friend not spoken up after a brief silence had passed between us.

"Do you think you should do it and just cry?" she asked, and even though we both knew the answer, I said it anyway.

"Yes, I do."

So I reached in my purse and grabbed the first bill I found, (unfortunately for the happy couple, it was $1), placed it in the jar, and danced with my brother. There are a lot of things I could have said in that moment with him, and you can bet I thought hard about it as we twirled around the dance floor to Journey's *Faithfully*. I wanted to send him off with some kernel of sisterly wisdom; some tacit statement that summed up everything we had been through. But as the song came to an end, I hadn't come up with anything, so I said goodbye to life as we had known it with the only thing that really mattered anyway.

"I love you," I said.

"I love you, too."

And there it is.

Love.

The reason I'm explaining all this in the first place. Because believe it or not, I think about this mail-order ring a lot. I think about it whenever I think of my brother and his wife and the way they have essentially grown up together, living from paycheck to meager paycheck and carving out a charming little life for themselves in which they have almost nothing they want but everything they need. I guess whether a studio apartment or a sprawling mansion, a tiny silver ring or a giant sparkler, love is still love.

And that's what I was thinking as they drove away from the reception that night, the getaway car dragging cans and other decorations. I was still trying not to cry, and my brother rolled down the window, looked right at me, and shouted out a silly movie quote we both love, and in that moment, I realized that I would always have him. And he me.

I was forever his, faithfully.

insights you didn't ask for

WHEN PEOPLE LEARN ABOUT MY BORDERLINE obsessive love of jewelry, their brows usually furrow into a look of severe confusion. It could be due to the uniqueness of the degree to which I care about all things gem (translation: I'm a freak), but it's probably more because I'm usually not actually wearing any jewelry. And when you hear someone proclaim themselves a jewelry aficionado, you probably expect them to be donning at least one or two sparkly baubles.

I *own* a lot of jewelry, so it's somewhat hard to explain why I rarely wear any. The simplest explanation, and it is absolute fact, is that I'm always running late and never have time to peruse my jewelry inventory to select the perfect piece for the day's outfit. I see people who do this—who put in this time each morning—and I confess I envy them. They make me want to be better; to make more of an effort with my jewelry. Like the woman in my office who has pieces in every color, rich blues and pinks and purples that she color-coordinates based on what she's wearing. They aren't real stones, mind you, and a bit too gaudy for my tastes, but I admire her forethought.

Another of my excuses for not wearing jewelry is that my life doesn't feel like it presents many opportunities for dolling myself up. Not that jewelry need be saved for fancy outings and festivities, but the thing about jewelry is that it's fancy by nature, and so it's not uncommon for me to save my own diamonds for those special occasions when I'm not at work or running errands or sitting at my writing desk. And since not much of my time is spent doing any other than those three things, my jewelry box is usually closed.

But here is another fact, and perhaps the root of the problem. As much as I love jewelry, even when I *am* attending an event that warrants some bling, after putting it on I am usually hit by the following thought: *Who am I kidding? I can't pull this off.* It's a silly and completely irrational thought, as any woman can rock a stunning piece of jewelry. Yet I'm sometimes overcome with the realization that on the spectrum of women in this world, I am definitely on the low end when it comes to glamour. A bit of a tomboy as a kid, I've never been what I would call girly, and even though business school and the corporate world forced me to up my style game, it is still very simplistic, my style, even down to my makeup, of which I don't wear much. So putting diamonds on my ears and around my neck can make me feel like I'm not myself, or like I'm pretending to be someone else.

When I do wear jewelry, there are two different styles I go for. The first is my "Here's Your One Chance, Fancy" look, or Fancy for short, and this is the look I go for when I do feel like dialing up my appearance. My Fancy look includes any of the pieces from my fine jewelry collection. Think gold and diamonds. Think expensive. These are the times when I throw on diamond earrings and a Tiffany necklace and bracelet for church. Or for a night on the town. Or because I have a work meeting with a snotty girl who probably doesn't believe that a person like me owns real diamonds and I want to show them off.

When it comes to my Fancy jewelry, I am single sourced. Other than my Tiffany purchases, everything has come from Carlton Jewelers. It's because I know them, I trust them, and it's important to me to support my hometown economy even though I no longer live there. The only Fancy item I own that didn't come from Carlton's or Tiffany, although ironically it's my most valuable piece, came from a store in Cleveland. I had won a $250 gift certificate, and while this is nowhere near what I'd need for a big ticket item, it's still a nice chunk of change. I perused the cases and selected from about five favorite pieces a pair of lever back earrings set in white gold. The diamonds were emerald cut, and each was surround by a rectangle halo of baby rounds. It's one of my favorite looks—I love it in oval and cushion cuts for wedding rings—because the halo makes the center stone seem bigger, plus the look is delightfully antique.

These emerald cut stones were by far the biggest diamonds I had ever looked to purchase, and the selling price of the earrings was more than I felt comfortable paying (especially when I hadn't planned on paying *anything*), but I rationalized that the gift certificate gave me a nice head start. Plus, I didn't really love anything else there, and as previously stated in this book, getting what you love and will wear often is so much better than saving a bit of money.

My second look when it comes to wearing jewelry is my "Triple Ique" look, ie. antique, unique, boutique. I'm single sourced here as well, because I was lucky enough to come across a line of jewelry creations at an arts fair while on vacation one summer, and I've never found anything I like better. I bought three pieces from this woman on the spot at her booth, and when I vacationed there again the following year, I contacted the woman to ask if her jewelry was available in any stores for me to purchase while I was in town. It wasn't, but this kind woman allowed me to come to her home and look over everything she had. I wrote a check for $300 and walked away with a dozen more pieces.

If you're wondering what's so wonderful about the Triple Ique look, think bronze-toned chains made to look worn and weathered. Think necklaces made from old watch parts, bracelets cut from vintage tin cans, and pendants cast from molds of old-style keys. It's a look that is more "me" than Fancy, so I'm more comfortable on Triple Ique days. Of course, it's a look that has become quite popular, especially in combination with geek chic glasses a la Zooey Deschanel. I know this because I now see jewelry like this at *every* arts fair.

As to what I would recommend for the average girl out there, I'd suggest you look around and find something that works for you, something you're comfortable with, something that won't require you to take on a second job in order to support. That said, every girl should still own a couple of Fancy items, because there will be times when you'll be glad you have them. But whatever you do, don't mix the two looks (i.e. I don't wear my Zooey Deschanel glasses with my Cleveland lever back diamond earrings), and for the love of all that is holy, do not leave the house wearing *too much* jewelry.

How do I know what is too much, you ask? There is no hard and fast rule, but keep in mind that if you find yourself wondering whether you're wearing too many accessories, you probably are. I once sat through the sales pitch of a very well-meaning woman who sold inexpensive jewelry from a catalog and she explained that eleven is the number of accessories you should put on before leaving the house. Hats, glasses, and scarves count toward the eleven as well, she explained, so it doesn't have to be all jewelry, but let me take this moment to tell you that if you leave the house wearing eleven accessories, I guarantee you look ridiculous. If you take nothing else away from this book, take that. And don't say I never did anything for you.

Fire rose

I'll never forget the day that the co-worker in the cube next to me at Pressure-Sensitive Leader asked for my help in brainstorming gift ideas for his wife.

"It's for our ten-year anniversary," he explained.

I knew this man pretty well, and I wasn't sure how his sweet wife put up with him. He didn't mistreat her in any way, but from what I'd observed, he didn't appreciate her—or their children—as much as he should. He was the guy who would always come to work even when sick because he actually preferred to be out of the house during the day; the guy who after telling us they could barely handle their three children seemed to go into a state of depression when his wife got pregnant with their fourth. His life (or his wife's life, rather) made me sad, so his interest in making their ten-year anniversary special gave me hope that even the lousiest of husbands can change for the better.

"That's great! When is your anniversary?" I asked.

"Today."

At this point it was already afternoon. On his very ten-year anniversary. And he'd only started thinking about a gift *now?* So much for changing for the better. Whatever. His wife was an angel and she deserved something substantial, so I picked up my lower jaw and offered a suggestion.

"Jewelry," I simply said.

He managed to produce a brochure—mailed from a store in the mall—and asked my advice on which pair of earrings he should get. I didn't like any of them, or maybe it's just that I don't like mall stores period, but I pointed to what I felt was the best option.

"Those are kind of expensive," he replied, and it took all I had not to slap him upside the head.

They were something like $239. And if you don't think the mother of your children is worth $23.90 for each of the years she's spent with you, or $59.75 for each of the children she's borne, then you don't deserve her.

The immediate issue here was, of course, the shockingly cheap nature of my co-worker, but let's table that for now. Because the real mystery to me is the number of men over the course of my life who have asked me for advice on what to buy for their significant others. Valentine's Day, Mother's Day, anniversaries, birthdays. No matter the occasion, men become spastic and frantic in gift-giving times. Maybe it's that men tend to forget about these important dates until the only options available to them are last minute, but mostly it's that a man seems to want opinions from other women on what *his* woman wants. I suppose on some level this does seem logical — if not somewhat stereotypically offensive — but it's always been a bit disturbing to me that a man could legitimately not know what to buy for the woman in his life. I mean, shouldn't you *know what she likes?* At least *one thing* she likes?

And that brings me to my point, which is simply this: If you're wondering what she wants, the answer is jewelry. It's always jewelry. I'd even go so far as to say you can never go wrong with jewelry, which shouldn't come as a shock to you when you compare it to other quick-hit gifts for females. Flowers? Pretty, but they wilt inside of a week. Chocolates? Delicious, but gone in a matter of days (or hours) and ultimately will leave her feeling bad about either her waistline or her lack of self-control. From a day at the spa to a weekend getaway to dinner at a fancy restaurant, most gifts you can think of are fleeting, and I can bet you that no matter how thoughtful the gesture, she'd rather be presented with something sparkly in a small, velvet box. Something that lasts forever. Like a diamond.

True, jewelry is universally appreciated by women (and hence a slam-dunk, will-get-you-lucky gift), but that's not its only appeal. The best part about purchasing jewelry is that it's so easy to buy. If you have a jeweler of choice, or even if you don't, a jewelry purchase can be as simple as walking into a store, asking to see some diamond stud earrings, and selecting the size that corresponds to your budget. A man can certainly put in more time should he choose to, but the bottom line is that a jewelry store is a one-stop shop for any and all birthday, anniversary, and holiday gift needs.

Holidays in particular were my favorite times working at the store. Not only are they prime gift-giving times already, but everything is also on sale, which further entices customers to buy. The holiday sales, Christmas in particular, were so much easier than all the others. The holiday itself provided a deadline, and the store would always be full of clueless men who just wanted to buy something pretty because they were running out of time. As a salesperson, that's exactly the kind of customer you want, because it's pretty much a sure sale.

Don't interpret this to mean that my glee at seeing a full store during holiday times was due to all the extra money it meant for me. Because Carlton Jewelers only paid me by the hour, which meant I made the same amount per day whether I sold one thing or twenty. Rather my glee was because I loved having so many willing customers. I loved the busyness that was such a refreshing change from the usual slow pace of purchases. I loved finding homes for all the beautiful things in our store. I loved guiding the customer through the entire process, from greeting him at the front door to gift-wrapping his purchase.

Mostly though, I loved thinking about all the women in town who would wake up on Christmas morning to find little, exquisitely-wrapped boxes underneath their trees. All the smiles, hugs, tears, and kisses. All the delight and admiration that these gemstones would bring to their owners over the course of a lifetime.

If you can look me in the eye and tell me that this moment—the moment when she looks at you in disbelief and throws her arms around you as she exclaims her delight, or maybe all the moments that follow as she cares for, cherishes, and looks forward to wearing the piece every time you go out—if you can honestly tell me you don't think that's worth $239, then I'll say it again: You don't deserve her.

Zinnia

Let's talk for a minute about platinum, which I would have none of if it weren't for—you guessed it—my Aunt Leah. Unlike the little red ring that caused visions of rubies and diamonds to dance in my head all the way up until Christmas, this platinum gift was a piece I had never even seen before. It was a total surprise. And one I wasn't entirely sure how I felt about when I opened the fancy leather jewelry case and saw its contents: a plain silver band. A far cry from diamonds and rubies, it seemed like regression personified. What had Leah been thinking?

It happened like this: Leah found herself at an estate sale and saw a 1940s platinum wedding band in the mix of available items. Seeming like something I would appreciate, it made her think of me. And this is all I really needed to know in order to forgive the lack of gem stones. Because the ring's lengthy past was instantly fascinating.

First of all, it has to be said: Platinum in and of itself is just sexy. It truly is the premium jewelry metal. In fact, on a recent trip to Tiffany & Co. in New York City, the salesperson took it upon himself to point out—after I had asked "Is this platinum?" for the tenth time—that Tiffany engagement rings are now set exclusively in platinum. More rare than gold, platinum prices have historically been up to three times higher than those of gold, a discrepancy that has only recently evened out. To reference this same trip to Tiffany & Co., I was shocked when comparing a line of necklaces to find that those set in gold were negligibly less expensive than those set in platinum.

Platinum also wears much better than gold, but I mean that strictly from a durability standpoint. Look at it this way. While it's easier to get a nice shine after polishing a gold band, the same gold band is not nearly as durable as its platinum counterpart. In other words, if my 1940s wedding band were made of gold, it would not have been preserved as well. Sixty-year-old gold looks more its age.

My platinum band was imperfect, mainly because one half of it was noticeably thicker than the other half. I liked the way it looked on the thick side better, so I'd always try to position it that way on my finger, but I've spent a fair amount of time over the years pondering how this even happened in the first place. Poor workmanship, most likely, either when it was originally cast or perhaps during a repair of some kind. Or maybe it had been a gradual transfer; maybe something about the way the previous owner had worn it or treated it, the rough environment it was exposed to. Although it's hard to believe anything could have been strong enough to have had that much of an influence. In any case, the ring had *been through something.*

Which is closer to the heart of why I love this ring so much and why it's spent infinitely more time on my hand than the Tiffany band mentioned in the opening chapter of this book. The platinum band had a history, and even if I knew nothing about what that history actually was, it satisfied the sentimental side of me even just to speculate. Hopefully some of you know what I mean and have likewise at some point wondered about the previous lives your precious possessions have lived, or, more appropriately, the lives their owners have lived, although I'm not sure there's a difference.

My favorite thing about the platinum wedding band—
and the ultimate evidence that it had lived another life—
was that it was engraved. Truly a lost art in today's society,
engraving is really the only way for future generations (or
random strangers who end up owning your heirlooms
sixty years later) to know anything about you, or to at least
know someone cared enough about you to craft a personal
and meaningful message.

It's like that Billy Collins poem about people who
write notes in the margins of books. Those books feel
lived in, and in many instances you can glean things
about these prior readers and their lives or temperaments
based on the lead scratchings left behind. ("Pardon the
egg salad stains, but I'm in love." Remember that one?
Swoon.) Or perhaps more to the point, engraving jewelry
reminds me of the handwritten dedications people
sometimes inscribe inside of front covers or on that blank
page that often follows. I haven't been around many old
books in my lifetime, but my best friend Ellie—who has
a degree in library science—has. She's always acquiring
old books, bags and bags of them, and she sometimes
takes snapshots of her favorite handwritten inscriptions.
I enjoy reading through them, because they represent
love, hope, and meaning in the lives of people I will
never meet but am perhaps not so unlike, even in a
world unrecognizably changed.

As for the engraving on my platinum band, all I can
make out after so many decades is the word "Sumiko,"

which I can only assume is a name. Either the first or last name of the original owner. There's also a date inscribed, although all I can read clearly is the word "June," (the sixth, maybe?) and that the year was nineteen hundred something. I don't know Sumiko, but I've thought about her a lot over the years. Wondered what her wedding in the 1940s was like, who she married, and why one of her children doesn't have the ring today. I'm sure the ring has seen things I can't imagine, but I like imagining anyway. I like having this type of connection to someone now moved on to higher and holier things. If in heaven she ever finds herself wondering where her wedding band ended up, I hope she sees it's with me and feels relief. I hope she knows I think of her every June. Especially on the sixth.

Dahlia

The average person doesn't know much about jewelry. They know about gold, might have heard about platinum, and can identify the colorless wonder seen in every store window as diamond, but that's about it. Or maybe I should give the general public more credit. At least the women, who tend to know a few additional details, such as names of stones and styles of cut. But the men in general seem to be limited to the facts I listed above, and it's amusing to me that the only thing more widely known about diamonds than their color-less appearance when compared to other stones is that there's a cheap replacement out there that looks exactly the same.

You show me a man who says he hasn't at least thought to himself that he wishes he could just put a cubic zir-conia in his fiancé's ring and I'll show you a man who's lying. And while some women may not be able to tell the difference, that's not the point. The point is that there is power in knowing you own the real thing; knowing that your man was willing to pony up because you're worth it. Not to mention, these two stones do actually appear quite different, as there are very real differences that even an untrained eye can identify.

What you probably don't know is cubic zirconia is not the same thing as zircon, a naturally-occurring mineral. Cubic zirconia is a synthetic, and is completely man-made. You could almost say that it's created solely for the purpose of synthesizing diamonds. This, however, doesn't mean that cubic zirconia is simply a synthetic diamond. It is a different substance altogether. This means that cubic zirconia is a fake; an imposter meant to take the place of something infinitely more beautiful.

Please don't misunderstand me as being anti-synthetic, because I am a huge proponent of the idea of the synthetic gem. After all, one of the hardest things about being connected to the jewelry business is that you know things you wish you didn't about the circumstances under which precious stones are mined. Not that you should look at every piece of jewelry you own and assume that it came to this country Blood Diamond style. But realizing the physically grueling nature of mining work, the danger that comes with it, and the political instability that riddles so many gem-producing countries, sometimes I do feel badly that so much goes into getting these stones, and that most people never even think about it. We just see something beautiful and assume it's always been sitting right there in a store window; cut, faceted, polished, and mounted to perfection.

I guess what I'm saying is that sometimes the idea of a gem that was simply grown in a laboratory is more appealing. But lest this appear as a contradiction to my dislike for cubic zirconia, let me remind you that a cubic zirconia is *not* actually a synthetic diamond. It has a completely different chemical composition. But as for gems that *are* synthesized with the exact same chemical compositions as their natural counterparts, I would have no qualms with owning one. There's even something fascinating about our ability to re-create the environments and temperatures necessary to create actual gemstones. It's so self-sufficient. So innovative. So MacGyver of us.

What this all means is that I'm not one of those people who turn my nose up at the thought of a gem that didn't come from the Earth. And like I said, I would have no issues with owning one, yet most of the time, I'd probably choose a gem that *did* come from the Earth. Not because there's anything phony about synthetics, but because there's just something better about gems that grew all on their own. And the more you learn about the specificity of the circumstances required to produce a particular gemstone, the more you will come to appreciate the real thing. Between the temperatures and elements and climates and geology, the crystal structures and growth patterns and chemical compositions, it's a wonder these gems form at all. But they do. And it's miraculous.

When talking about synthetics, the other topic that usually creeps in is that of treatments, most of the time to either improve color or reduce inclusions and flaws. Much like synthetic gems, people tend to shy away from the idea of a gem that has been treated. Again, I agree that there is something enchanting about the idea of a completely unaltered, natural stone, but there are a couple of key reasons why, much like synthetics, I have no qualms with treatments and why you shouldn't either.

First, gemstone rough looks like crap. Really, it does. And I'm not just talking about the cutting and polishing necessary for faceted jewelry. I'm talking about the characteristics of these just-from-the-earth stones. Take topaz, for instance, which is usually either colorless or a horrid shade of brown. If you're itching to purchase a pendant the color of orangey dirt, go ahead, or just buy the same pendant in a beautiful shade of pale blue. Yes, it's true that blue topaz is actually colorless topaz that has been irradiated and then heat treated, but the blue is much more attractive, and I'd choose it every time.

The second thing to keep in mind about treatments is that they make gemstones on the whole much more affordable. Because if everyone insisted on buying only untreated gems, there would be a lot more demand for a lot fewer stones. Prices would skyrocket, and you'd find yourself unable to compete. Take emerald, one of the most popular colored stones in existence. Emeralds are probably the most heavily-included gems around. They are usually riddled with fractures, which is why I can pretty much guarantee that any natural emerald you own has been fracture filled. It's a process that fills existing fractures with a clear polymer or resin, and it significantly improves the overall appearance of emeralds. Since no one wants to own a cruddy-looking emerald—but no one wants to pay an ungodly amount for one of the few good-quality natural ones out there either—what treatments do is bring attractive emeralds within financial reach of the general public.

So please, dear reader, don't reject treated or synthetic gemstones simply because they grew in a lab or aren't sold in their natural shade of puke. Learn to appreciate the slew of professionals who held the stone before you did and made the series of decisions that transformed it into the most beautiful version of itself.

Trillion

A perk that comes with working in the jewelry industry is that even though it's a retail environment, you seldom have to deal with upset customers. As arguably the hardest substance on earth, it's not as if diamonds break, and so jewelry in general is very unlike other industries in this way. Sometimes I think about all the electronic gadgets I've bought that broke sooner than expected or about all the clothes I've returned that didn't fit properly, and I have to imagine that working in the customer service areas of these types of businesses must feel a lot like hell.

This is not to say that jewelry doesn't require some amount of maintenance—restringing of pearls, re-enforcing of prongs, replacing of heads—or that problems don't result when such things are neglected. Because they absolutely do. Jewelry must be maintained. And while it's difficult to accomplish, it *is* possible for stones to crack, for metal to bend, and for chains to break. So it's not that jewelry never needs fixing. It's just that the overall process of wear and tear when it comes to jewelry takes a very long time. It simply lasts longer than almost anything else you can buy.

What this means is that people rarely become upset with jewelry stores over their purchases. They seldom ask for their money back (although a woman might want to exchange something her husband bought for her), seldom have quality complaints, and seldom bitch to you about how they were treated unfairly during the process of a sale. There are really only three potential problem areas for jewelry stores.

First—and this is a big one—there's been an alarming increase of instances where customers are not told the whole story at the point of sale. I'm talking about jewelers who fail to disclose or who are dishonest about details such as the stone's origin or value. Some people are even sold fake stones altogether, and they have no idea. If this happens to you, know that you have every right to make a fuss, and you can and should march back in to your jewelry store and let those bastards have it.

Second, and I promise I'm not making this up, jewelry stores sometimes unknowingly blow a man's cover when he's sleeping with someone other than his wife. Here's how it happens. Man meets girl. Man likes girl. Man sleeps with girl even though he is married. Man continues on in this fashion and eventually buys a piece of jewelry for his mistress. The store mails a thank you note to his house, as is customary for many, and his wife sees it and comes running down to the store in a complete rage. The wife actually going to the store is somewhat confusing, in that the store itself isn't to blame for the affair. Just know that this happens, and that regardless of the actual presence of fault, the store will be perceived forevermore by these women as an accomplice.

Finally, we can't ignore the fact that disaster does sometimes strike the store. I'm specifically talking about damage done during even a sometimes routine repair. Some stones are of such low quality that they cannot withstand repairs. Some stones are delicate by nature and can't handle the heat from a torch or steamer. And sometimes jewelers and goldsmiths simply mess up. Whatever the reason, it's possible, although very unlikely, that your precious piece of jewelry might not be returned to you in the same pre-repair state. This is the hardest problem area to deal with, because people are insanely attached to their jewelry. And you will find yourself unable to be calm, rational, or profanity-free if this happens to you.

In my time at Carlton Jewelers, I can only remember one person who ever became genuinely upset. This woman was having us design a ring for her, and since Steve didn't actually design or make rings in house, the design center in another state that we sometimes utilized was the one actually doing the work.

When you are having a ring completely made from scratch, the designer will cast a sample ring with which to get your approval. It's usually made out of a blue, waxy substance and is of course meant to show you what your ring will look like when finished. The tricky thing is that blue wax looks nothing like precious metals, and it can be hard to manufacture the mental adjustment needed to picture what the blue wax will look like when silver or gold. Add to that the fact that it's always hard to articulate the ring you want and see in your mind, and this can turn into a rather frustrating experience rather quickly.

The day I saw the lady lose her cool in the store, she had come in to see the latest version of the wax mold that the design center had mailed us. There had been several versions before this, and she had sent each one back. No dice. As she stood at the counter and held her wax-clad hand out, she didn't like what she saw once again. The frustration became too much, and almost as soon as she reacted she was apologizing for being so unpleasant. In one of Nancy's finest moments, she assured the woman that she had every right to be frustrated; that it didn't matter how many times we went back to the design center; that the most important thing was getting this ring right.

And we did. Eventually. Another satisfied customer. Which is exactly my point. When it comes to uniting women with diamonds, it's hard to go wrong.

Emerald

I don't consider watches to be pieces of jewelry. They are far too practical. They are battery operated, for crying out loud. And they actually serve a purpose aside from looking nice or being a mere accessory. Not that some of you out there don't own watches purely for their good looks or for the status and power associated with luxury brands (you know who you are), but most of us wear a watch for practicality's sake alone. We just want to know what time it is.

Of course when I say we, I mean you. Because I have never been a wearer of watches. On second thought, I take that back. I remember being quite smitten as a child (read: also as an early teenager) with a Mickey Mouse watch I had. Most of my life up to that point had been spent living in California, and I was consequently obsessed with all things Disney. It's the same reason why I wore a ring bearing a flat, painted Mickey Mouse head during that same time period. Mickey and I were *tight*.

Even though I haven't lived in California since I was nine, I still view Disneyland as the ultimate treat; the place I love visiting more than any other. I dream about being there so often that my dream self now knows I'm not really there, and I'm horribly let down even before I wake up. Clearly you can't take the Disney out of the girl, but there did come a point in my childhood when I lost interest in the Mickey Mouse watch.

Prior to that point, however, I milked it for all I could. None of my friends had watches that I recall, or

at least not any featuring such an iconic character as
Mickey Mouse. I viewed the watch as something that
might elevate my social status. It would give me a chance
to brag about Disneyland, and it would perhaps even
generate a bout of watch envy among my peers. Eventually I realized that no one in town really cared about
Disneyland, and more than that, the reason no one wore
watches is because there was absolutely nothing cool
about them. *Hey, guess what guys? I know what time it
is.* Or, *Oh, so you're more popular than me? Well, I can
tell you exactly how many more minutes of recess we have.
Bam!* Plus there's always a morning in every girl's childhood where she wakes up and realizes, as if some sort of
instinct has suddenly kicked in, that one of her fashion
choices is gravely misguided. Or all of them.

There are two reasons why I don't wear a watch. The
first and much more relevant reason is that the need for
time-telling devices in this technology-heavy world we
live in has drastically decreased. When I think about
my average day, there is literally not a moment when
I'm more than a glance away from knowing the time as
it is. While at work, the time is staring at me from the
bottom right corner of my computer screen. And if all
the pixels in the bottom right corner of my computer
screen were to suddenly short out, I can always glance
just past my computer to my desk phone, where the
time is posted at the very top of the display screen.

While in a meeting, I'm carrying my cell phone and

can check the time as needed. On my drive home, the clock on the dashboard display screen is as easy to see as my speed. Easier, actually. And if I were the type of person who cooked dinner, it's nice to know that both the oven and the microwave have clocks that are always on display.

The situation I'm describing isn't unique to me, for I'd wager there's not a single moment in the day that the majority of us don't have our cell phones handy. So what's the point of having a watch?

Unless you like the way it looks.

This, though, is the other problem I have with watches. I don't think they look particularly good. Again, they are not jewelry. And especially for women, the positioning on the wrist is a bit of a lose-lose. When worn low and close to the hand, it doesn't look quite right. But when worn higher and with a few inches of space between watch and hand, it doesn't look right either. There doesn't seem to be a sweet spot. And I think thicker-banded watches look better, which is why men can get away with wearing watches more than women can.

This lack of affection for watches doesn't mean that I didn't still have a favorite watch picked out at Carlton's. It wasn't because I truly had a desire to own one, but the frequency of slow days always found me in want of something to occupy my mind. A decision to make. An object to consider. A trinket to covet. *Anything*. Plus, watches took up a significant amount of space in the store, so it's not as if I could ignore them.

And they weren't all bad, the watches. I admit to admiring the boxes they came in, by far the most official-looking packaging of anything in the store. The boxes looked like wood (but obviously weren't) and the faux-graining was polished and shiny. Big enough to fit a watch and also leave plenty of cushion room, the boxes were a sight to behold in the wall case that held them, each one open at the hinge, watch propped up to allow customers a peek at the contents. I could have bought one just for the box it came in, and on several versions of my Things To Purchase Before the End of Summer list, one watch in particular usually made the cut.

The band was metal as opposed to the fabric or leather variety, and it was slightly thicker than the majority of women's watches at the time. The face was square shaped, and my favorite thing about the watch was that the surface of the metal had a brushed look to it. It wasn't shiny, and the whole thing seemed more palatable. I didn't really want the watch, but it was my favorite one we had, I could get it at a discount, and if I was ever going to wear a watch at any point in my life, reasoning suggested I should just buy it. And so it stayed on my list all summer as I waffled back and forth on what to do about this whole watch business.

In the end I opted to go without it. There were far more sparkly things on my list and the watch couldn't compete. But perhaps I'd have made a different decision had there been a Mickey Mouse watch in the bunch.

I can see it on the wrist of my dream self, having just come from a face-painting booth and waiting in line for Mr. Toad's Wild Ride.

Radiant

One of the most fascinating things about studying gemology is it becomes apparent just how many different avenues in which there are to work. And all under the umbrella of the jewelry industry.

As for me, I'd really only ever thought about being a jeweler. Either the kind like Steve who runs his own store, knows the clients, takes the trips to Antwerp, and repairs the jewelry, OR the kind who just repairs the jewelry. Because let's not forget that my core interest in a jewelry career was the jewelry itself. So even though I loved sales and could easily picture myself building relationships with the citizens of a community through running their local jewelry store, I could just as easily see myself exclusively working on their jewelry. I wouldn't get as much customer face time if I were a bench jeweler, also known as a goldsmith, but sometimes the idea of sitting in a back room sizing rings and re-setting gemstones all day sounded nice. I'd spend my days making beautiful things more beautiful, shiny things more shiny, and of course fixing what had been broken. Either way, being a jeweler felt like a good fit. It always had. But then again, I hadn't known at the time just how many other options were out there.

Not until I actually made the decision to go to jewelry school did I learn that the gemologist degree—not the bench jeweler—was the one I should probably go after. It was more prestigious for one thing, although that alone wouldn't have been enough to sway me. The kicker was that becoming a gemologist opened up so many more possibilities when it came to actually learning about the gemstones I'd be working on. And especially since the beauty of gemstones is what pulled me to them in the first place, I really did want to learn about them. As much as I possibly could.

Being a gemologist carries with it some definite perks, most notably that you don't necessarily have to open your own store. With so many different ways out there for people to receive their training, complete apprenticeships, and acquire stores, it's not all that uncommon to find a jeweler who is not a certified gemologist. And who consequently needs one. You can then be hired by a store owner to be her official gemologist.

I know people who have done just that and who now do the official appraising and grading needed for the stores at which they work. Big name jewelry chains hire gemologists in much the same way, or they might pay on a more ad hoc basis, requesting a gemologist's presence only once or twice a month, at which time he hammers out all the appraisals that have been piling up. Some gemologists make their living doing this exclusively—traveling around between various jewelry establishments taking care of the things that require gemologist certification. It's not a bad gig, really, and it's a skill set for which there is obviously a need.

Speaking of needed skill sets, my studies soon revealed exponentially more jewelry career options out there. I was shocked at how many people were employed by this industry. Just take pearls, for instance. There are entire families who do nothing but run pearl hatcheries. It's risky business, one that can be wiped out completely by weather or water plagues like red tide. Imagine that, your entire crop or harvest gone in an instant. Not unlike the risk associated with produce growers and farmers everywhere.

Owning or working for a hatchery might not be feasible or desirable for those wishing to get involved with pearls, but from buyers to wholesalers, pearls offer an interesting opportunity for those who base their careers around them: speciality. Pearls are a bit sepa-rated from other gems, by everything from appearance to formation, and those who focus exclusively on them become all the more specialized. And speciality is key, particularly when people base their purchasing deci-sions—whether a single pearl or an entire parcel—on how well you know your stuff.

The same could be said for specializing in any gem, and that's what makes the jewelry industry so big. For every kind of gemstone, there are buyers, wholesalers, and retailers. For every kind of gemstone, there are miners recovering it from the earth. For every kind of gemstone, there are sorters and polishers. For diamonds in particular, there are entire labs filled with graders doing nothing but assigning grades. There are cutting centers in Thailand, New York City, Antwerp, China, and Israel. Not to mention the marketers whose task it then is at the end of all this to effectively market the stones through various taglines and campaigns.

There are also the institutions doing all this teaching in the first place. Educational establishments like the GIA. Think of all the people employed there. It's a thought that occurred to me as I was sitting in a GIA classroom one day, and the part of me that loves teaching combined with the part of me that loves jewelry thought it actually sounded like a pretty ideal gig. There's much more I haven't mentioned, but hopefully you get the point, which is that there's a lot more to the jewelry industry than the jeweler selling you a ring from her inventory.

But the one job I wish I had more than any other in the jewelry realm is that of a gem cutter. I've heard Meg Berry talk about what she does and seen her walk an audience through the pieces of rough she's worked on that have been her favorites, and to me, this is the winner.

The winning slice of the industry that combines the power of transformation with the skill of mathematical precision and yields the ultimate satisfaction of creating something beautiful.

If I could have my way, if I could go back in time and start again on a career path, that is the one I would want. It wouldn't come without stress, for I'd wager there isn't a cutter out there who hasn't at some point botched the optimization of a good-sized chunk of valuable rough, but figuring out the best way to utilize gem rough—taking into consideration everything from shape to size to location of inclusions—would in my mind be the ultimate puzzle. Plan, cleave, brut, polish, presto. A setting-ready stone. From what came in looking like nothing more than a rock.

Sometimes it's hard to admit that if you could go back, you'd do it differently, but for most of us, this just goes with the territory. The territory of life. And I'm no exception. Yes, if I could have my way, that's what I'd do. I'd be a gem cutter. So if you need an apprentice, Meg, let me know. I'll be waiting by the phone. Practicing my laser skills.

small town bling

WHEN WORKING IN A SMALL TOWN, YOU ARE bound to encounter people you know on a regular basis. This is unavoidable. It's simply a statistical fact that when the population in your area is low, the odds are much higher that the customer walking in the door is a former classmate, a neighbor, the man who delivers your mail, or the woman who teaches water aerobics at the pool whose body you secretly wish yours looked like.

There are various responses the world over when you run into someone you know in a setting that has nothing to do with the context in which you know them. Some people view such run-ins as fortunate occurrences that allow for catch up and chit chat. Others high five or shake hands, some even hug. If bad feelings exist, many people choose to ignore or even publicly snub the other person. Me? I prefer to walk the other way with my head down and hope the person doesn't see me.

I don't know why this is, other than perhaps some sort of gut reaction based on my own introversion or a natural flight response when I'm afraid a chance interaction will put me on the spot and force me to instantly produce details about my life and circumstances that for some reason are harder to voice when I hadn't planned on doing so.

Whatever the reason, the truth is that I do not enjoy running into people outside our normal circle of interaction, and however silly, I still feel this way even as a grown woman in my thirties. On a recent trip home to Oregon for Christmas, I was at the public library and could tell even without looking that the woman who had just come in and approached the front counter was one of my teachers from junior high. One who had always vouched for my high academic abilities even though all I ever really did was turn in my assignments and behave myself. Still, I knew I had made an impact on this teacher all those years ago, and running into me and hearing about my life almost two decades later might have warmed her heart. I knew this, yet I walked out of the building as stealthily as possible.

The same thing happened on a recent trip to a high-end grocery store. I saw a woman who had previously worked in my office, but I couldn't at first convince myself to approach her. When I finally let out a "Hi Stephanie," from a ways behind her in the check-out line and she didn't respond, I scurried to another line feeling rejected.

I don't share this with you as an illustration of my social shortcomings, although I'm sure you've gotten the picture, but rather to illustrate how uneasy I sometimes felt when faced with the possibility of someone I knew walking through the door of Carlton Jewelers. Because let's face it, making a beeline *away* from customers has never been an effective sales technique.

It's a bit of a paradox that I felt this way when selling to people I knew, because throughout my whole life, I've always had the heart of a salesperson. Not in a shady, have-I-got-a-deal-for-you kind of way, but in the sense that connecting people to things they want and need gives me a tremendous amount of satisfaction. *Especially* people I know. There's really nothing about selling itself that I inherently like (think cold-calling, aggressive or pushy styles, wining and dining a la an old-school boys club). But if there's a way for me to use my connections, company, and resources to give you something—a product, a service, a solution—that makes your life easier or better, then I will want to do whatever I can to make it happen.

The most logical explanation for why I tended to dread helping someone I knew at the jewelry counter was that despite my content (and borderline glee) at being able to call Carlton my place of employment, sometimes it struck me as, for lack of a better term, beneath me. Not that I didn't love it, but I worried about what people would think. How it would be perceived. I mean, it was retail. And not everyone who came through the door was someone I was thrilled about having to serve and wait upon and, when occasion called for it, flatter incessantly.

And even though I knew it was only temporary, there was also a part of me that felt like a failure on some level. Especially when I ended up back at Carlton even after graduating from college. *Here she is folks, our very own valedictorian, newly matriculated and…back home working retail for minimum wage? Wait, that can't be right.* Except it was. I honestly had no idea what to do with my life, and so I hated when people would come in the store and ask me to answer that very question. But there wasn't much I could do about it, and so as people poured in and out all summer, I got used to it.

Of all the familiar faces who doubled as customers while I worked there, three experiences stick out in my mind, the first of which was a watch I sold to Mrs. Kennedy, the woman who taught my sex education class in high school. Not that anyone teaching sixteen-year-olds can even hope to actually teach them anything about sex, but I have all the fondness in the world for Mrs. Kennedy. Not for the sex lectures, but for being such a wonderful and down-to-earth woman.

I was actually happy to see her when she walked in, and after all the time I spent with her in selecting the watch, when the time came to purchase it, she resolutely told me she wanted to make sure I got the commission, even if it was someone else who rang up the sale. I appreciated the gesture far more than she could have known, as that kind of salesperson/customer loyalty is hard to come by, but I kindly informed her that none of us worked on commission, which, all things considered, probably only helped my income.

Another customer I won't forget is a man I actually hadn't seen before. He was looking at wedding bands, no doubt to give his fiancé some idea of what to buy for him. This wouldn't fit into the category of waiting-on-people-I-knew at all, except that I found out after the fact (when she showed up to collect the ring) that his fiancé was none other than Mrs. Kensington, my star of a freshman English teacher.

When she came into the store and I made the connection, she told me the whole story, including the circumstances that led to her recent divorce. When discussing this divorce with a few fellow teachers at school, another teacher passing by heard the tail end of the conversation and threw a "You too?" at Mrs. Kensington, for it turned out he also was going through a divorce.

That the two of them went on to fall in love struck me as so hopeful that day when she told me. And it still does. Not in a second chances kind of way, but because what had happened to her was so incredibly sad and awful. The kind of thing that happens to you and you are almost completely sure you will never be as happy as you once were. *Okay*, maybe. *Not depressed*, maybe. *Pleasant and positive*, maybe. But not truly happy. Not ever. So seeing someone get to that place after such a blow is among the most satisfying things we can witness on this earth.

And finally, speaking of weddings, a memory I'll for some reason always keep was the day I saw a former high school classmate of mine, a year or two younger than me, at the far end of the cases looking at engagement rings. Turns out he was planning on proposing to another classmate of ours, a girl I had acted with in one of the high school musicals. She was a lovely girl, very nice, and this boy, Tommy, was equally wonderful.

Tommy had actually become a baptized Christian a few years earlier, and as a member of the same congregation, I had enjoyed seeing his spiritual progression and how happy it made him. He didn't have a very solid situation at home, and I gathered that religion brought a lot to his life.

As I neared the end of high school, Tommy stopped coming to church. It just wasn't working out for him, although I gathered it was a choice he felt he needed to make in order to keep other areas of his life in harmony... or at least to keep them from falling apart completely. But I also gathered it was a choice he wished he could have avoided altogether, or at least that he wished his choice could have been different. The reason I respected Tommy so much, and still do, is that when asked if his decision meant that he no longer believed, he said it didn't. Not at all. "I know what I felt," were his exact words. And for a teenage boy to be that sure about anything in life seemed even in the wake of his decision to be a small miracle.

And so my heart warmed seeing him in the store. Little Tommy, in love. He was nervous, probably about the purchase as much as the proposal. I was flooded with thoughts as I contemplated the future for him and his bride. They surely had no money, no plans, and he was having me show him the bands that had literal specks of diamond. Not more than $100 or $200 dollars. I thought about all the obstacles these teenagers would encounter as they embarked on their life together, and while part of me wondered how this was a good idea, the bigger part of me knew I could go my whole life and never hear of a better one.

That's the thing about love—and that jewelry is at all tied to love is one of my favorite things about it, by the way—it's a gamble, see. Anyone who's ever been in love can tell you that, and the ones who haven't could tell you the same thing, since more often than not, they've been unwilling to take those gambles.

You always hear people talking, speaking of Christianity, about how fear is the opposite of faith; how you have to dispel your fears before faith can develop. Others say the opposite of faith is doubt, as it's simply not possible to both believe in something as well as waver. Of course, people who say either of these things are ridiculous, because I've spent my whole life being perfectly faithful yet simultaneously scared shitless about how everything's going to shake out someday.

The only way you can avoid being scared on some level is if you know something for sure, so if you want to know what the opposite of faith is, it's certainty. Neither Tommy nor Mrs. Kensington knew whether their impending unions would work out, and for every pair of clueless nineteen-year-olds who stay married there is a mature couple divorcing after decades together. You simply never know. All you know is how you feel now. Today. While looking in a jewelry store window, thinking about the person you love, and wondering what they've got planned for the rest of their life. My suggestion would be to take the gamble and ask them.

Marquise

Let me tell you a few things you might not know about a jewelry store. The first is their reliance on a product we all know and love: Windex. Yes, Windex was a part of my daily—no, make that hourly—life at Carlton Jewelers. It's what we used to clean the outside of every case and counter, a task which I completed sometimes countless times throughout the day. Partly because fingerprints are pesky and are left after virtually every customer, and partly because selling jewelry in a small town is a slow business, so oftentimes I ended up cleaning all the cases and counters even if they didn't really need it. I hated having nothing to do.

It's safe to say I became so accustomed to the smell of Windex that I grew rather fond of it. Which is sick. But nevertheless, I found myself spraying more than necessary and then leaning over the counter and sniffing until I realized how disgusting it actually smelled. Which always took longer than it should have. Did I mention how sick this is?

A second use for Windex, and this one might surprise you, is that of a lubricant when rings get stuck on people's fingers. And this seems to be a common problem, one for which I've heard of many remedies, although none as feasible as Windex for a store setting. Think about it. What would you do if your jeweler pulled out a vat of butter from a fridge in the back and slathered it all over your hand as you stood at the jewelry counter? I can tell you what *I'd* do, and it would not involve making a purchase. How much simpler it is, and less messy, to simply reach under the counter and pull out a bottle of Windex and have the ring off after a couple of squirts. Remember that the next time you end up in this predicament. Or knock yourself out with the butter, but don't say I didn't warn you.

A lot of people wonder about security when it comes to jewelry stores, and let me assure you that the safe is every bit as intimidating as it seems. I never knew the combination or had any idea how one would actually go about opening it. There was never any reason for me to know, as I was never in the store without either Steve or Nancy. All I did was help unload the trays of goods each morning and then pack them back up and re-load the trays into the safe at the end of the day. I enjoyed the unloading and set up much more than the take down and re-loading, because it was morning, because the store wasn't yet open, because the day had such promise, and because it was time which we could dedicate wholeheartedly to getting things ready. Take down bothered the compulsive part of me, because we started about forty-five minutes before closing time. Which meant that a customer could walk in right in the middle of it, and you'd have to try and help them even though half of your inventory had already been loaded back into the safe for the night.

In terms of security itself, I never felt unsafe at the store. It was a small town and there was a police station relatively close by. I thought about it plenty though, and my writer mind sometimes ran away with me because I had no idea what I would actually do if someone walked in and started waving a gun in my face. Besides crap my pants.

There was only one customer who ever gave me any

legitimate fear, and much to my dismay, he was not an infrequent visitor. Sometimes I swear it was like he lived on the streets right outside the store, which might actually have been the case, since I was never sure whether he had an actual home.

A loud and obviously mentally unstable man with unkempt, shoulder-length brown hair, he would come barreling in and tell me and Nancy about whatever was going through his head that day. I seem to remember frequent mention of some sort of female super hero (She-ra, was it?), and I was never sure if he thought he was dating her or if he was just really obsessed with her. At some point I think he actually started paying for a cheap ring, like a dollar or two at a time, and this was sweet (a ring for She-ra!), but his visits were always unsettling. Not that I think he ever would have hurt us, but I didn't know, and if anyone was going to come in and rob us blind some Tuesday afternoon, this was the guy.

Steve always seemed to be at the Taber Glen store when this man showed up, so Steve told me very firmly that I was to call him whenever the man entered the store. Not sure what good it would do to have Steve on the line while the man blew us to smithereens, but I called him each time the man showed up. Nancy playfully chided me years later for the speed at which I would disappear to the back room at the first sight of the man, but hey, I had my orders.

The window displays were one of my favorite things at the store, and I'm still relatively obsessed with them no matter where I go. If I pass a jewelry store, I will slow down and hug the glass as I walk. It's because I want to see the jewels, naturally, but it's also because I like seeing how the jewels are being showcased. The clever slogans, the elaborate props, the beautiful decorations, everything positioned just perfectly within the case. At Carlton we removed the actual pieces of jewelry from the display windows each night, which must have been somewhat disappointing for evening shoppers who happened to pass by.

If you want to know the truth, I would love to have been part of the display creation at Carlton, but I was a peon. Not to mention I had exactly zero creative ability when it came to fluff and decoration. But I loved watching the window displays take shape, largely due to Nancy's efforts, and I looked forward to seeing what each new month would bring to the window. Three-stone diamond pieces one month, Armani collectible porcelain figures the next, then black pearls, then back to diamonds, maybe a designer we'd recently picked up. Given that a jewelry store's inventory stays relatively constant (big ticket items don't exactly fly off the shelves), the variety of the window displays filled my need for change.

And finally, speaking of inventory, you might be interested to know that it's not uncommon for many of the wedding rings in a jewelry store to be filled with cubic zirconia rather than diamonds. It's not a scam, it's just good business. At least in terms of total inventory dollars. Because mixing in some CZ among your bridal rings allows a jeweler to bring more items into her store, as there's less money tied to each piece. When a customer wants to purchase one of these rings, the jeweler simply replaces the CZ with a diamond of the customer's choosing. Usually the customer has sat with the jeweler and selected the combination of clarity, color, and carat that best aligns with his budget.

I could usually tell which rings at Carlton contained CZ instead of diamond. They were the biggest stones in the store, and you can tell when you look at a CZ, especially if it's big, that the fire you see doesn't even compare to that seen in a diamond. Everything is just a little more open and blank. But for those of you at home who may not feel as confident in your ability to distinguish between the two, just look at the price tag. If it's going for a ridiculously low price—like jump up and down and thank your lucky stars low—plan on having to add in the price of a real diamond. And plan on having some Windex on hand. In case you ever need it. Come to think of it, stores should really give away a bottle with each purchase.

I can smell it now.

English round cut

The general assumption when a man buys an engagement ring is that the girl to whom he gives it will say yes. They've either talked about it and developed some kind of understanding, or at the very least, he's thrown out a few vague "what if" musings about their future life together and has received enough positive feedback to prompt him to seek out a reputable jeweler.

The easiest proposal approach—I call it the Slam Dunk—occurs when the couple has talked at length about marriage. In many cases, they've already decided to get married, and the proposal happens after the fact, usually some epic gesture involving either a crowded public event or an ungodly amount of roses. I'm not sure at what point in modern history that a proposal ceased to refer to the moment the question is asked and the decision made, but whenever the shift occurred, the pendulum hasn't yet swung back. Because a proposal in today's terms is still usually defined as the moment in which the ring is given, even if the couple has already decided to get married.

It should come as no surprise that in the case of the

Slam Dunk approach, the woman is typically very involved in the selection of her ring. She has accompanied her boyfriend to numerous jewelry stores, and after long afternoons spent hovering over cases and a few sit-down chats with jewelers about Antwerp quality and the four Cs, she has either selected her favorite ring or at least left her boyfriend with a clear idea of what she wants. He can then come to the store on his own, purchase her dream ring, and plan his proposal. Even though his girl totally knows it's coming.

The more challenging approach is what I call the Leap of Faith. The man in this scenario doesn't already have a committed bride, and while he and his girlfriend may be a long-established, deeply in love couple, the M word has not been specifically discussed. This man will pick out a ring completely on his own and surprise his girlfriend one night with a bona-fide proposal. He'll get down on one knee and ask her to marry him while holding the little jewelry box with shaky hands. She'll cover her mouth in disbelief and utter a series of exclamations that start as surprise, morph into excited hysteria, and eventually settle into overwhelming emotion.

As a woman, I'm much more fond of the Leap of Faith approach, and much more respectful of the man with the balls to use it. The Leap of Faith is so much more honest and raw. It's the kind of gesture that says, "I'm not sure if you're as crazy about me as I am about you, but this is how I feel, and I'm asking you right now, in this moment, to make a decision that I think you already know you want to make." Not that I've thought about it or anything.

The selling point of the Leap of Faith is that you'll never get a truly sincere and unrehearsed reaction from the Slam Dunk approach. On the other hand, I suppose with the Leap of Faith you're not actually 100 percent confident that she'll say yes. You're pretty sure she will, you can't imagine her *not* saying yes, but you don't actually know she will.

Yes, as a woman I prefer the idea of the Leap of Faith, but as a lover of jewelry, I can't quite stomach the thought of leaving the selection of my wedding ring up to someone else. Even if I love him dearly. I could end up with a yellow gold band supporting a giant zirconia stone, or a diamond mounted in his really fat grandmother's ugly setting with baby peridot stones flanking the sides. *The absolute horror.*

A variation of the Leap of Faith approach is the Double E Leap of Faith approach, the Es standing for Extra Effort. This happens when a man wants to surprise his bride not only by proposing to her, but also by presenting her with a ring that he himself has designed. There's a certain sweetness in a man becoming this involved with the process, a certain enhanced confidence he usually possesses about both his girlfriend's jewelry preferences and the likelihood of her saying yes. Of course, there's also a certain foolishness in a man who knows nothing about jewelry thinking he has any business trying to design it.

A Double E Leap of Faith man is hard to find—probably the *real* story title that Flannery O'Connor was after—and in my summers at Carlton Jewelers, I only ever ran into one. A striking young man with dark hair, I'd never seen him before when he came into the store and shook Steve's hand one afternoon. It was obvious this wasn't the first time they'd met, and while I could tell their topic of conversation was somewhat serious, I couldn't imagine what it was.

Intrigued, I inched my way closer to Steve and the dark-haired man and heard enough of the conversation to gather that the man was hoping Steve would buy back the ring he had purchased. Steve had custom made it based on the man's own idea for a design and was explaining that the best he could do would be to pay the man for the scrap value of the gold, which would only be a fraction of the purchase price. Steve looked pained, the man looked even worse, and it suddenly dawned on me what had happened. The man had proposed and the girl had said no. Now here he was stuck with this ring and no fiancé.

The man left the ring with Steve, most likely to let him estimate its scrap value, and I wandered into Steve's workshop as soon as I got a chance. I wanted to see this ring. This poor, rejected ring. I turned the job envelope upside down and a simple, slender band fell into my palm. White gold embedded with alternating diamonds and sapphires, it was certainly understated, but it was also classic, and I developed an immediate fascination with the ring. Although something told me it was the ring's story and not the ring itself that had me fascinated.

Then I saw a note written on the job envelope just under the man's name. It explained that the ring had been designed for a girl named Raegan Hall. I couldn't believe it. I *knew* her. A girl I graduated from high school with, Raegan Hall had at first been somewhat awkward with her glasses and voluminous laugh, but after moving away for a couple of years, she returned to Taber Glen with contact lenses and a sudden beauty that was nothing short of stunning. She was still odd and her laugh hadn't changed, but there was a presence about her that was new.

Before I knew it I had slipped the band on my finger. Standing in Steve's workshop at that moment wearing the ring that could have been Raegan's, I wondered what it would be like to have a man who wanted to marry me. I wondered how the unfortunate conversation between Raegan and her boyfriend must have gone down, and why she hadn't said yes when he knelt before her with his darling face and his own custom-made creation in hand. She must have had a reason. Because here's the thing about women: We want the Leap of Faith. But only *when* we want the Leap of Faith. For there are few things more awkward than being proposed to when you aren't yet sure this is the man you want to marry, or worse, when you've recently begun to realize that you don't think he is.

The trick for men when it comes to proposals then is to plan on taking their girlfriend by surprise, aka the Leap of Faith approach, but only when they're certain she would say yes. This may seem an impossible task that defies logic, but what exactly about what women want has ever been the least bit logical?

Exactly.

Cushion (old mine)

A jewelry store can seem pretty out of place in a town as small as Taber Glen. A town where the largest structure on Main Street is a saw shop; an inexplicable building of such gargantuan size, it makes one physically stop and ponder how such a cavernous inventory of saws could possibly be finding homes.

If you were to drive down Main Street, the saw shop would be the first thing you'd see, followed by an optician's office, a mini-mart, a gas station, a shady-looking motel, a tavern that may or may not be operational, an insurance agency, a St. Vincent De Paul, a bank, a Mexican restaurant, a gift store specializing in stuffed bears that I cannot believe has stayed in business, the Elks Lodge, a real estate office, and—always the apple of my eye—a Dairy Queen.

The few avenues branching off of Main Street house a hardware store, a fitness center, what I think is another mini-mart, a barber shop, another bank, and several antique stores that somehow manage to sell nothing that is either antique or even desirable. And nestled into the right side of Second Avenue is Carlton Jewelers. Or at least it was until they closed the store some years ago in favor of the newer store in Pinetell, but for all the decades it stood there, it was a beacon of fancity among the regular small-town humdrum.

It's not just the town being small that made a jewelry store seem out of place, it's also that the overarching industry was timber. A large percentage of Taber Glen's population were employed by one of the surrounding lumber mills, and based on my own observations, lumberjacks are not the most likely group of people to frequent fine jewelry stores. And don't assume it's all on account of money, because you'd be surprised how much many of those jobs pay. I think it was more of a mindset. Diamonds just aren't thought of very often in a timber town come gift-giving time. And not all women are like me. Some see no need for fine jewelry, or, particularly when living in a small town, feel they have nowhere to wear it.

Even though I'm not convinced money was always

the reason people didn't patronize Carlton Jewelers, there's no denying that the economy was depressed, especially when a mill closed. If you didn't have a job, it was hard to find one. If you had a house to unload before you moved, it was hard to sell one. Because no one was moving in. There was nothing bringing anyone to the area, and unfortunately, this is still the case. Only now there are even fewer mills open and the economy is even more depressed. Aside from the family who owned the gas station and apparently had oil money, there really wasn't any notable wealth to speak of, yet somehow Carlton had survived in Taber Glen for over four decades.

Pinetell I was less familiar with as a city. True, we went often enough for orthodontist appointments and school shopping and an occasional movie in the theater, but it was so much bigger that I could never recite the Main Street lineup like I just did for Taber Glen. I simply didn't know it that well. I didn't even know if they *had* a Main Street. The only part of the city I ever became very familiar with was the oldish downtown area where Steve put the new Carlton store. I drove the twenty-five-minute route every day to work, exiting the freeway a few miles early in favor of a side highway that spit me out on the edge of the downtown area.

Keep in mind that I'm talking about a downtown more in the historic realm and less in the modern, busy, professional hub realm. Pinetell's downtown area was never crowded, and in addition to several Mom and Pop type restaurants, I remember there being a drug store, a Hallmark store, a bank, a post office, a sports supply store that specialized in adhering lettering to shirts and jerseys, another jewelry store (much less sizable and glamorous), and an engraver's shop. This is not nearly all, but it's all I can remember. Like I said, I was far less familiar with Pinetell.

It's worth noting that all of the streets in downtown Pinetell were one way. The absolute bane of my existence. I remember Mr. Stratfield taking us through these streets as part of our Drivers Ed training, and the whole ordeal had me completely frazzled. Navigating downtown meant you had to have a pre-existing knowledge of which streets ran which way. When I didn't, instead of being able to calmly deduce from either the posted and clearly marked signs pointing right or left or, I don't know, maybe *the direction of any cars passing by*, I would arrive at an intersection in a complete panic. I would waffle the steering wheel back and forth until deciding to take my chances in a direction, and then scan the street for any sign that I'd made the wrong decision. Like the headlights of oncoming traffic. Not sure why one-way streets had the ability to wither me so. It was the same thing that happened in school when I'd get called on unexpectedly. The capacity for rational thought simply vanished.

Not that it took very long to master the directional

grid in a downtown area as small as Pinetell's, and Carlton's was, lucky for me, positioned on one of the far ends of the grid, which made each trip there seem less obstacle-riddled. I was clearly putting myself and everyone around me at risk every time I encountered one-way streets.

The Pinetell store was much more extravagant than the one in Taber Glen ever was, and part of this was because Pinetell had such a downtown area in the first place. Like I've said, the space Steve rented was positively made for a jewelry store, and the charming feel of Pinetell's downtown—although I'm not sure it ever felt to anyone as charming as developers at one point surely thought it would—gave the store's image and appearance an additional boost.

Speaking of boost, the clientele at the Pinetell store had more money to spend, or maybe it's simply that there were more people period, and by extension a greater number of people with money to burn. Sort of how there might not actually be more smokers per capita in New York City—even though it sure seems that way—just more people, and consequently more smokers.

Still deep in timber country, fine jewelry wasn't the best fit even for a cozy little downtown like Pinetell's, and sometimes I feared our attempts at fancy window displays and pretty posters to pull people in off the streets were futile. We even planned a special after hours event one night where—get this—wine would be served. Wine! Poured from bottles! Served in glasses! And sipped while perusing cases of diamonds! You could not have found a more classy event that night in the whole county, and in spite of myself, I looked forward to it with much anticipation. And that's saying something, considering it meant working late. And, much to my chagrin, I was too young to even serve the alcohol. I was simply on hand to help man the rush of customers who would be flooding in as soon as business hours were over. And I couldn't wait to bask in the presence of Pinetell's finest.

As it happened, I'm pretty sure I could count on one hand the number of customers who came in that night, and what a shame it was. Not just for all those unopened bottles of wine, but for the let down of there not being enough upscale people in Pinetell to carry off such an event.

The only couple I knew of who had actual money, and apparently lots of it, (and yes, they did attend the wine event that night) were frequent visitors of the Pinetell store and were responsible for one of the most elaborate and involved projects Steve ever did. The wife had acquired a lot of jewelry over the years, and she decided one summer to have everything she owned re-appraised. Or maybe some of it had never been appraised in the first place.

She brought in all the pieces, several dozen of them,

inside plastic sorting compartments. Almost like giant pill-dispensing strips that give you a place to put each day's medicine, these contained rows upon rows of compartments, each one filled with a piece of jewelry. A necklace, a ring, a pair of earrings. We kept the plastic compartments in the safe, and Steve spent entire days doing nothing but appraising them.

As a side note, the whole concept of appraising seemed slippery to me then, and in many ways, it still does. On one hand, appraising is simple. You determine a stone's characteristics and then match those against current price lists to assign a value. But grading those characteristics is more subjective than you might think, and other factors—like the ever-fluctuating price of gold—could make an appraisal inaccurate in almost no time at all. Re-appraising then becomes a must.

Which I suppose is why Mrs. Wealthy was having Steve do all this in the first place. And while most of the items in those compartments were too gaudy and colorful for my taste, I loved having them in the store. I loved thinking about how much she must have trusted us to let us temporarily house her entire jewelry collection. I loved seeing each finished appraisal as it spit out of the printer, complete with a picture of the item and a thorough description of its characteristics and value. But mostly I loved knowing that somewhere in this region was a couple wealthy enough to buy jewelry and classy enough to drink wine.

Split-brilliant

You can thank Tiffany & Co. for putting Tanzanite on the map. Or on the market, I should say. Personally, I find the story fascinating, but that's because I'm a jewelry buff.

Tanzanite is most often classified as a royal blue stone, but I've always thought it looks more purple than blue. At any rate, it's officially made of the mineral Zoisite, and you can imagine the popularity it gained with a name like *that*. Granted, it wasn't entirely about the name. There were certainly other factors affecting consumers at the time of the blue/purple stone's debut, some having to do with the part of the world where the stone originates, and some having more do to with supply issues.

In any case, it was Tiffany & Co. who took on the repositioning and marketing of this gemstone, discovered in 1967 in Tanzania, not far from Mount Kilimanjaro. Tiffany named the stone Tanzanite, and while this was certainly not the first stone with a name that paid homage to its place of origin—Andalusite, Hiddenite, and Tsavorite to name a few—as far as marketing goes, it was a genius move. The name Tanzanite hints at its exotic birthplace, and combined with a campaign that emphasized the equally exotic and rich hue of the stone, it suddenly appeared to consumers as much more desirable. Tanzanite is still by no means what I would call a popular stone, but it's regarded highly, considered extremely precious, and continues to demand a premium in price. I'm not sure Zoisite would have been able to say the same.

A similar story unfolded several years later in Australia, home of the Argyle mine. The world's largest diamond source by volume, the Argyle mine is a big deal. Their claim to fame is their pink diamonds, of which they produce upwards of 90 percent of the world's entire supply. But when they found themselves with a stockpile of recovered brown diamonds, they needed a strategy for moving them. Not a problem unique to the Argyle, surely, as brown is the most common of all diamond colors. And no one ever wanted them. Who would? They are *brown*. The color of dirt. And poop.

So the Argyle, clever little mine that it was, started marketing these castoffs using words like "champagne" and "cognac." And even though the color of the diamonds was just as poopy as it had always been, suddenly they were seen by consumers as palatable. Even desirable. For there's something alluringly sexy about the pairing of diamonds and bubbly, and hats off to the Argyle for thinking of it. Even I—a person who doesn't drink and has never been particularly enchanted by brown diamonds — now find myself pausing to linger on display windows containing diamonds in a soft brown color. And when staring at those displays, *champagne* is all I can think. It makes these diamonds seem not at all like the second-class castoffs they once were, but as something that I would actually feel more classy for owning. Now that, my friends, is marketing at its finest.

Advertising for an average, run-of-the-mill independent jeweler doesn't have such a scope. Steve wasn't responsible for introducing a new stone or creating worldwide demand, but he *was* responsible for creating in the local population enough desire for purchasing jewelry to at least keep him in business. No small task in this particular corner of the world.

When talking about advertising, marketing, or general tactics that are meant to increase foot traffic, the most obvious and simple way to accomplish this is to temporarily reduce prices. That's right folks, a sale. Anyone who sells anything knows what happens when people find out they can get something at a discount, especially if there's a limited window. Particularly in the jewelry market, where the items are so costly to begin with, you'll have almost constant foot traffic on the days where, say, everything is twenty percent off.

Twenty percent was the standard discount offered at Carlton Jewelers, and we tended to pair it with peak jewelry-buying periods to further entice people into the store. Think Christmas, Valentine's Day, and Mother's

Day. Twenty percent seems like a pretty healthy discount, but remember we're talking about an up to 300 percent markup, depending on the jeweler. I didn't at the time have any basis for comparison to know if our prices were in line with others in our area or field, but I'll never forget the day my mother stopped by the store and made the mistake of talking prices with Pamela.

"I'm waiting for the big sales," is the gist of what Mom told Pamela on a non-sale day.

"Well, we have our prices set low from the start," Pamela replied, probably a bit annoyed at Mom's assumption that sale prices were the only ones reasonable enough to pay.

What Pamela may not have realized was that a sale was the only way my mom could afford to purchase anything, period. Low prices or not, in a small town, they always needed to be lower. It's the reason why my dad charges pennies for animal immunizations and surgeries. And it's the reason why non-sale days at Carlton were slow as all hell and sale days sometimes impossible to keep up with.

We did things like posters out on the sidewalk, displays in the windows, and, occasionally, commercials on local TV or radio stations, but my favorite advertising campaign Carlton ever ran came in the form of a gamble. At least on the part of the store. Prior to the kickoff of the Christmas season one year, Carlton announced that if we got at least two inches of rain or snow on New Year's Day, then customers would get a refund on their Christmas purchases. *The intrigue!* A chance to essentially get jewelry for free! Nevermind that the chance for snow in Oregon is zilch and the odds of that much rain on January 1 are slim to none. That didn't matter to me. I loved the whole idea. Because however small, there was a chance.

This introduced a whole new level of excitement amongst customers that December, not to mention a whole new element of risk for the store. So much risk that I wondered whether it was wise. Wouldn't promising to refund more than a month of sales require that you be absolutely certain that whatever you're betting against doesn't happen? And we were talking about the *weather*. Not exactly something synonymous with certainty.

I expressed concern about it one night at home, and Dad assured me they must have thoroughly researched it and had it on good authority that this year would not bring a torrential downpour come January 1. But no matter the history of every prior January 1, there was no way to guarantee that this one would follow suit. Despite various almanacs and projections, it was impossible to look ahead that far and know how much precipitation to expect on a certain day.

I guess what I'm saying is that I was panicked. For the store. And however confident Steve and Pamela were, they had to have been at least slightly worried. Can you imagine having to refund every single purchase from a busy Christmas season? What a blow that would have been. And so I held my breath that holiday season, and much to everyone's prediction, there was no significant precipitation on New Year's Day.

After all that worry, I was surprised that what I felt that day wasn't relief, but rather disappointment. Apparently I'd begun rooting for the weather just to prove everyone wrong. In any case, it's the most invested I've ever been in a sales tactic. And I still check the weather report in Oregon every New Year's Day. I'm telling you, one of these years it's going to happen. I hope it's the year I've finally splurged on two carat studs from Antwerp.

Oval

Let's turn our attention for a moment to the salespeople at Carlton Jewelers. To quickly review the cast of characters as you know them so far: Steve, the jeweler, didn't work the floor much because he was usually busy either meeting with clients at his desk or in the workshop doing repairs. Pamela, his wife, would work the floor if it was busy or we were shorthanded, but most of the time she would keep herself busy in the back or up in her office. Nancy, the store manager, who's already been described in other sections of this book, was the one I worked with the most, but she wasn't always at the store. Nor was she the only other salesperson at Carlton.

Let's start with Maisy, who let me just say right now is one of the most glamorous people I've ever known. Her blond hair, which had to have been artificially colored (or perhaps artificial altogether), was always styled into a high poof, and she was always impeccably dressed. Her age I could not even begin to guess, although I wouldn't be surprised if she had at that time been in the ballpark of sixty. Since she didn't get many hours at Carlton, Maisy's main job was a salesperson at a local department store. Perfumes, make-up, high-end clothing. From what I knew of her, it seemed a perfect fit.

Maisy wasn't married, and I knew absolutely nothing about her love life. Being an attractive, well-dressed woman, she was probably not in want of gentleman friends, but I could be wrong, and I always felt a little sorry for her regardless. She struck me as the type who put a lot of effort into the way she looked, perhaps as a way to land herself a suitor, yet there she was, alone.

There was something dramatic about Maisy, and just to give you a taste for her glamorous flair, picture this: On one particularly slow day, Maisy stretched herself out, come hither style, on the antique chaise at the front of the store and perused the store's coffee table picture book. By way of comparison, I had never seen any other store employee even sit down on that chaise, let alone sprawl out.

"This is the *longest day of our lives!*" she suddenly exclaimed, still on the chaise, and I think she really meant it.

In reality, it was just another slow day, but the intensity in Maisy's voice as she said those words has stuck with me, and whenever I'm having a particularly hard day, I picture her stretched out on that chaise with her head thrown back in exaggerated desperation.

Cynthia on the other hand was very much the opposite of Maisy, in both personality and glamour. Cynthia lived just down the road from me, and one of her five children, Andrew was his name, graduated in my same high school class. Andrew was a harmless boy who for some reason made me constantly uneasy. He'd had a locker near mine and was always trying to figure out my combination. He'd sneak up behind me and watch me as I turned the lock around, and sometimes I'd catch him standing at my locker attempting to open it based on what he'd seen over my shoulder. I'm not sure why the thought of him actually opening my locker horrified me so, but I managed to make it all through school without him figuring out the combination. I remember being quite pleased with myself when on the last day of high school I taped a note on his locker that said nothing more than this:

Andrew,
My locker combination is 24 – 14 – 36.
Tali

Cynthia was a quiet, calm woman, and I liked her because she reminded me of my mom. Someone who had raised several children, someone who didn't have much experience working outside the home, and someone whose appearance teetered on the plain side. Not because she was without beauty, but because just about anything was more important to her than clothes, hair, and makeup.

And like my mom, Cynthia also had a daughter who had been involved in theater in high school. She'd had the lead in *Kiss Me Kate* the year I was in the seventh grade, and at the time I thought she was so talented, I went to see it four times and made it a goal to one day be in her shoes on a high school stage. Locker-spying Andrew was not without musical talent if I recall, although there was only one year where we were able to convince him to join the school choir.

Steve and Pamela's younger son, Tim, worked in the store one of the years I was there. He was energetic and personable like his father, although the jewelry business certainly saw him out of his element. Tim was a theater man, only he'd gone beyond high school and actually made a career out of it, although I gathered it was slow-going. He'd been in New York City for a while, but was for some reason back in Oregon that year, and he wasted no time in organizing a local production of a new off-Broadway show that I found to be an absolute treat when I went to see it.

Out of all the salespeople, Barbara was my favorite. She only worked on Mondays, and her no-nonsense, down-to-earth attitude was refreshing. What you saw was what you got with Barbara, and I loved hearing the stories she would tell me on slow afternoons. A strong woman, I think she may have had a hint of Native American in her roots, she had battled cancer and survived.

A dark-haired woman with small, thin lips, Barbara loved her time in the store, and she, like me, always liked having something to do. She'd busy herself with polishing or dusting while we talked, which is something you would have never seen Maisy do. And on her birthday every year, Barbara left flowers on her parents' graves, without whom she never would have been born in the first place. To this day, it's just about the sweetest gesture I've ever heard.

Of course, all these people could easily write a section about me in their own memoirs, and I'm sure I gave them lots of material in the arena of being clueless. I was shy, didn't know much about our inventory, suppliers, or, for that matter, about jewelry. And for all the customers who walked into Carlton Jewelers during the time I worked there, I was surely the least capable of handling their requests. But they employed me anyway, treated me as one of their own, and gave me the chance to do something I had always wanted to do. A classic case of them meaning much more to me than I ever meant to them, but I can live with that. At some point, every girl has to.

confessions

THE ONLY TIME JEWELRY EVER BROKE MY heart was when I was studying pearls. I'd always been fascinated by them, and not just because they could be counted among the rather selective list of organic gems. Rather my fascination centered predominately around the fact that they grow inside of a living animal. There's something inherently special about that.

Perhaps it all started in junior high when we read John Steinbeck's classic and utterly tragic novella, *The Pearl*. While I knew it was a moving tale (our English teacher was openly weeping as she read us the heart-breaking conclusion), what my thirteen-year-old self picked out of the story was that pearls must be very valuable, and, more importantly, very rare. I think that's what had me so enchanted; this idea that pearls were not a guarantee. That you would, in fact, run into them very rarely even if you spent your days doing nothing but shelling mollusks. This introduced some amount of fate, luck, and even destiny when it came to the topic of discovering pearls. Despite the demise of little Coyotito, I was hooked.

When I first heard of *cultured* pearls, I immediately bucked the idea off, kicked it in the crotch, and ran away at full gallop. Cultured pearls? The word suggested something grown in a laboratory, and I assumed that someone must have come up with a way of growing fake pearls that still looked like the real thing. Which was simply sinful. Because what makes a pearl so endearing is that it grows inside a mollusk. On its own. And it's either there or it isn't. Who wants a guaranteed, shiny imitation grown out of a petri dish? I sure didn't, and I never gave cultured pearls a second thought. Until I began my formal study of jewelry, that is, and realized that I couldn't have been more wrong about them.

See, a pearl grows when an intruder or irritant of some kind burrows its way into the shell of a mollusk. In response to the intrusion, the mollusk secretes layer after layer of a substance called nacre, and the layers of nacre coat the intruding object and ultimately form into the lustrous spheres known as pearls. So all one would need to do in order to guarantee a pearl would be to manually place an irritant or intruder of some kind inside a mollusk's shell. And that is exactly the process of pearl culturing. It doesn't mean growing white circles of various paste-like substances in laboratories. It means essentially stacking the deck with regard to pearl production by implanting intruders (usually small spherical beads) inside of mollusk shells. And while learning of this interference did take away the element of fate and luck that had me so enchanted, I think I could have been fine with that. Cultured pearls were still legitimate. But I kept studying. And it got worse.

The first alarming thing in my study of cultured pearls came in the form of the abalone mollusk. They, believe it or not, have a type of hemophilia, and even the slightest imprecision with the scalpel during nucleation, the process by which the spherical bead is implanted, can cause them to bleed out and die right there on the table. This fact caused me to actually pause from my studies for a few minutes. These poor hemophiliac abalone mollusks. The risk for harm being so much higher, I decided right then to take a stand. I would never purchase any jewelry made from abalone cultured pearls.

But then another thought crossed my mind, one that ultimately proved to be more disturbing than the plight of the little hemophiliac victims: What's this business about scalpels? Can't you just open their shells a crack and toss the bead in?

The answer is no, you cannot. The nucleation process is actually much more complicated. It involves making an incision in the mollusk's mantle or gonad, placing the starter bead inside (along with a tiny square of mantle tissue from a donor mollusk), and then sealing the incision with some of the mollusk's own mucus. Translation: This is major surgery. Surgery that takes a few months of preparation as pearl farmers try to slow the mollusk's metabolic process as much as possible to reduce its potential stress. Surgery that then takes a few months of closely-monitored post-operation recovery time before the mollusk is placed back into its regular habitat. Surgery that the majority of mollusks—over fifty percent—don't even survive. Did you hear what I said?? *The majority of them don't even survive nucleation.* And I'm not just talking about abalone mollusks. I'm talking about all mollusks for all pearl types. And this changes things.

Even for those that do survive the surgery and successfully grow a cultured pearl, another percentage of them won't make it through the harvest procedure. In the case of Akoya pearls, the mollusks are all sacrificed at harvest. One hundred percent of them. And despite the overwhelming demand that necessitates the continued presence of cultured pearl farms and hatcheries, I just can't embrace them the way the rest of the jewelry world does.

This may seem strange and even somewhat inconsistent given that I am not opposed to the slaughtering of animals for the sustenance of mankind, but I don't seem to recall anything in the book of Genesis indicating that part of man's dominion over animals includes our desire to wear shiny things at their expense. The only way that the concept of a pearl hatchery seems acceptable to me is if it's partnered with a restaurant or seafood company that's using the mollusk meat anyway. Although regardless of what they do with the meat, the idea of breeding, raising, and then killing mollusks for the sole purpose of getting pearls still makes me feel icky. I think it always will.

I've also had people ask me why the so-called dark sides of other gems don't get under my skin the way that this pearl business does. *What about blood diamonds? How can you support the diamond market at all?* While I am certainly sensitive to these issues, I've always been much more affected and disturbed by the mistreatment of animals than I have by the mistreatment of humans. Animals are so much more helpless in this world, and the small ones without any speed, skills, or fight are entirely reliant on the hand they are dealt by humans. Which, if you ask me, is an enormous responsibility for us.

And while diamonds are forever tainted by the small percentage that come to this country blood diamond-style, it is on the other hand a virtual *certainty* that any Akoya pearl you own, see, or peruse in a store means that a mollusk is dead. It's just a different situation, and one of which I'm much less tolerant. Does it mean I won't carry pearls if I have a jewelry store someday? I'm not sure. Does it mean I won't wear my pearl jewelry anymore? Eh, I probably wouldn't go that far. But does it mean I won't be buying any more of it now that I know what I know? Yeah, I think it does. Call it a quirk, call it a stand, call it insane. It's just something I haven't been able to get past. Which is usually what happens when I read Steinbeck.

Trapeze

When I heard about a ruby and sapphire seminar being held on a Sunday afternoon in a fancy hotel ballroom just outside of Cleveland, I almost didn't sign up. Because who was I kidding? True, I had begun a formal study of gems, but only just barely. It's not as if I actually knew much about rubies and sapphires at that point, and the event was obviously geared toward jewelry professionals.

But pulling at my heart were the rubies and sapphires themselves. And if they were going to be in a fancy hotel ballroom just outside of Cleveland, then that's where I wanted to be, too. I would fake it as best I could around all those jewelers and gemologists, pretend that I had every reason to be there. Or *any* reason to be there. No one had to know that I wasn't really going for the seminar itself—which was a presentation meant to keep us updated on current treatments and pricing—and that I was really just there to spend some quality time with the gemstones. To see them, to look at them, to hold them via tweezers and rotate them under the backlight of a microscope.

By way of confession, spending time among the stones wasn't the only reason I wanted to attend. Because as I went through the process of registering for the seminar, I learned that the group sponsoring the event was the Ohio alumni chapter for the very same jewelry school at which I was currently enrolled. Only in the beginning stages of coursework, I hardly felt like an alum, but the group welcomed me warmly, and before I knew it I had not only registered for the seminar, but also become a member of the chapter.

And how valuable such a chapter suddenly seemed. Think about it. I now had access to jewelry professionals all over the state! Professionals who had been through the same schooling I was just beginning, who could answer my questions and offer advice, who could perhaps even provide potential sources of employment as I looked to switch careers once my schooling was complete. My hope going into the seminar, then, was to make some jewelry connections in the Cleveland area. Yes, to network.

Too bad I'm terrible at networking.

Not that it was entirely my fault. The event, other than the kickoff luncheon, was not very conducive to networking. It began with the presentation itself, given by a man and woman who were experts in the field of corundum. They showed slides and charts to explain the importance of keeping up to date with current pricing and then turned the focus of the presentation to the recent changes in treatments. After the presentation, we were directed to the microscopes throughout the room, each of which were stocked with individually-bagged rubies. The rubies at any given microscope had all been treated using the same method, and when you'd had your fill of the method—or become able to identify its characteristics—you moved on to another microscope, another method.

And so you see what I mean about networking. From presentation watching to microscope hopping, my only chance for actually conversing with anyone was the luncheon. Which is why I sat down next to a few women who looked about my age. Other than an older woman who had brought what looked like her teenaged son (maybe he was learning the business?), we were by far the youngest in the room. I had grand intentions of being chatty, of asking all kinds of things of these jewelry girls, of being friendly, or of at least introducing myself, but as soon as I sat down I lost my nerve. *I knew nothing. I offered nothing. I would leave with nothing.*

Luckily one of the girls eventually asked me about myself, and while I wouldn't say I actually networked or achieved my goal of establishing some gemological connections in the greater Cleveland area, I did learn enough about these girls to have the following thought: *You are living my life.*

They all worked at the same jewelry store, most of them gemologists just like I was studying to be. They asked me questions about my schooling and my interests and gave advice on everything from the different campus locations to the order of courses they most recommended. I found them very helpful, and the best part was hearing about their lives. One girl was married to a goldsmith, which actually caused me to internally swoon. Not because I'm set on marrying a jewelry man, but because of how charming the whole thing sounded. He'd sent her off that very morning after asking which tools she would need for the day. And the thought of being married to a man who could run down a gemological checklist—a la "Loupe? Tweezers?" etc.—made me smile. And they had a one-year-old daughter, which made the whole thing seem even more enchanting. I don't even know why. But they were a family. A jewelry family. And while I've always had a hunch that I'll want to quit whatever job I have as soon as I become a mother, I think jewelry is the one thing I might love enough to keep doing even with a baby in the picture.

Among the most valuable information I gleaned

from these girls—other than that I'd better not plan on finding a husband in the industry, as most jewelry salespeople are women and most customers, though male, are looking to propose to their girlfriends—was a glimpse into what my jewelry future might hold. Not that I could see myself becoming a full-fledged gemologist like they were. I couldn't. That was part of my sheepishness when it came to this entire endeavor. I wasn't sure what, in fact, I could do with a gemology degree but no actual experience with gems. And then the girl married to the goldsmith said something that pulled me up by the gut, buoyed my heartstrings, and permanently changed my outlook.

"You know," she said, "people with business degrees and jewelry knowledge are exactly who places like Tiffany hire to manage their stores."

Managing a Tiffany store. Now I could get on board with that.

Pipe dream as it may have been, it was enough to fill me with confidence and purpose about my reason for being at the seminar in the first place. I could add value to this industry yet. And so I stepped up to those microscopes with gusto and looked at as many stones as I could before time ran out. I honestly couldn't see any differences between the treatment methods, but then again, I wasn't really looking for them either. To me they were all rubies, all beautiful, all perfect, and all I wanted for the rest of my career.

Lozenge

Jewelry is a funny thing. On one hand, gemstones are beautiful. And it should come as no surprise to anyone that jewelry is the first thing I notice about a person. Particularly rings, as they are the most visually accessible. Family, friends, co-workers, people sitting next to me on airplanes, it doesn't matter. If I know you, if I've so much as run across you at some point in my life, I've checked out your rings. More than that, I've made a hasty judgment call as to the kind of person you are and if I wish, because of your jewelry, that I were you.

On the other hand, the beauty of gemstones depends in part on the appearance of the wearer. This wholeheartedly discriminatory comment is not ungrounded. It comes from a lifetime of observing jewelry and the people who own it. It really has nothing to do with how attractive a person is. For even if you know the ugly stick intimately, any beautiful jewelry you own will still manifest itself as beautiful when you wear it. It's more an issue of age, because the older we get, the more protruded the veins in our hands become. You know what I'm talking about, and it's not flattering. It's also unavoidable. Aging is such a bitch.

But life is one cruel irony. And much like couples who can only afford to build their dream homes later in life when their children have all moved away and they no longer need the extra space, there are also couples who use this later-in-life affluence to finally drop some cash on a few spendy pieces of jewelry.

The aging factor is one reason why I'm a firm believer in treating yourself to nice things throughout your life, and not just while in retirement. I'm not suggesting breaking the bank, going into debt, or bidding on items at a Christie's auction, but I think a big part of feeling like a million bucks while wearing beautiful jewelry is being young enough to still feel beautiful yourself. And this is perhaps why I always have such an urge to wear pieces of fine jewelry. Because I *am* young, and now is the time to enjoy it.

Since I didn't have a dazzling sparkler of my own while working at Carlton Jewelers, I would often wear pieces from our inventory around the store. If you ask me, it's an excellent sales tool. Girls perusing jewelry cases tend to be drawn toward "live" rings verses those just sitting in display cases. Why else do you think they try things on? And so I'd pick out something shiny, usually one of the two-carat Claude Thibaudeau creations, and watch the girls' eyes as they followed my hand around, and their faces as they found themselves wishing to own something so beautiful. One girl in particular seemed downright affected by seeing me in a two-carat sparkler.

"Someone must really love you," she said, still looking at the ring.

And in that instant, I recognized myself in her. Because that's exactly my thought process when seeing someone with a stunning ring. The girl hadn't been happy or excited when she'd said this to me, rather she'd used a tone that every bit said, "I wish someone loved *me* enough to buy a ring like that." Notice that her wistful remark hadn't actually brought the ring up at all. Because she wasn't actually talking about the ring, now was she? It's not always about the ring. Sometimes it's about wanting the *circumstances* that would cause a person to own such a ring. And that's exactly where my mind often goes when I see a ring I wish I owned. Although I suppose this logic doesn't always hold up. Take Vanessa Bryant.

Of course, wearing a ring in the store isn't the same as wearing one out in the world. Perhaps this explains why I took a ring from Carlton Jewelers home with me one night. It was just for one night, and it wasn't as if this sort of thing didn't happen. I knew for a fact that Nancy herself had borrowed a necklace and earrings set for one of her kids' graduations. The difference was that she'd probably gotten permission, and the item she chose to borrow was not worth over $5000. Mine was.

Yes, my $5,000 ring was a good-sized platinum-and-diamond band. It was one of my favorites in the store, and while my life as a twenty-year-old college student spending the summer at home in a small timber town didn't exactly yield any opportunity for showing off such a ring, I did have tickets that night for the summer musical put on by the local community college. And dammit, for once, *I* wanted to be the real-life woman who made all the others think to themselves, "Someone must really love her." The kind of woman I myself might run into and whose life I could then spend a few distracted minutes shamelessly coveting.

But most people aren't like me. I doubt anyone at the performance even noticed I was wearing the ring, and by the next morning, it was back in its case at the store. Still, I lived a dream that night; the dream of wearing a beautiful diamond ring, outside of a store, with hands bearing veins that were not at all protruded.

Table

I once bought a ring for a girl.

No, no. Nothing like *that*. She was a college room-mate my junior year, and, believe it or not, the ring had been part of a plan to save her life.

I'd been nervous to learn that one of my three room-mates that year would be a freshman. I became even more panicked when I learned upon meeting her that she was anorexic. Openly. Admittedly. Unabashedly. I suppose we would have figured it out based on her sickly-thin frame and her habit of dishing her food portions via measuring cups, but being so forthcoming with the news of her eating disorder always struck me as odd.

She, Beth, was also a cutter, another fact she had no problem sharing with us. Since she didn't like to come to church—and when she did she sat stone-faced and mute and looked at the floor—I often wondered why she had chosen this particular university in the first place. The majority of the people on campus were all of the same Christian faith, and it's not as if skipping church regularly was something that could slip by unnoticed.

It struck me early on in the semester that having Beth as a roommate was a blessing in disguise. Being surrounded by so many faithful, moral, and straight-laced people over the course of my college years had left me little opportunity to serve, help, or influence anyone. And sometimes a girl just wants to pitch in. So I took it upon myself to get to know Beth, to make sure she felt welcome and comfortable in our apartment, and to help her work through her issues.

My plan had a flawless beginning. I began spending time with Beth, talking about her life, her choices, her opinions, and quickly found out that she was as interesting as she was insightful. When she explained, for instance, that Jesus had actually committed suicide for not stopping his killers when he certainly could have, it just about blew my mind. This girl was deep.

I suppose you could say the plan began derailing when I started making changes to myself and my own life to make Beth feel more comfortable. I began eating less, for instance, so she wouldn't feel self-conscious over her small portions. I began occasionally staying home from church with her so she wouldn't feel like her absence was being judged. I began throwing in a few untruthful details about my past so that she wouldn't think I was as straight-laced as I appeared. And just to see what it felt like, I grazed the inside of my forearm with a knife. Just the one time. For the record, I felt nothing. Except extreme confusion over why anyone actually cuts themselves on purpose.

Perhaps it was all the time I had been spending with her, perhaps it was the weight I lost, or perhaps it was my overwhelming desire to see Beth get better, but at some point, my plan backfired. I hadn't become a cutting, anorexic, non-religious person, nor do I believe I ever would have, but I was in a bad place. I began seeing a therapist who concluded that while I was not depressed, I was suffering from a codependency on Beth, in that I was so obsessed with her needs that I wasn't taking care of my own. In my effort to help her, I'd made myself and my own quality of life worse.

As Beth became even more extreme in her rebellions and habits, I became even more determined to save her from them. So when she began threatening to kill herself, I had no choice but to be equally extreme. She needed a gesture, a statement, something sincere and loving to snap her out of this ridiculousness and remind her that she was an important part of many lives. Most notably, of course, being the lives of her family members. I'd never met them, but I knew they loved her dearly and worried about her incessantly.

That's what was going through my head when I went to a local jewelry store and had them manufacture a thin white gold band bearing a single tiny amethyst stone. Amethyst was Beth's birthstone, and, meant to remind her of the people in this world who were glad she was born, I had hoped the ring might ward off any future impulses to off herself. Which is exactly what I told her.

While it's true that my friendship with Beth was at that point already strained, I would never have guessed that she wouldn't want the ring. But a few days after giving it to her, she left the little jewelry box in my room with a note saying she couldn't accept it.

Beth giving the ring back isn't what upset me. What upset me was the essay she wrote for an English class later that semester that basically depicted her roommate proposing to her. I don't think Beth knows I read it, but I did, and I've never been so hurt in all my life. True that we had become close and I had undoubtedly grown attached in my quest to see her become healthy, but our friendship had never been anything romantic, and neither had the ring gesture. And she knew that, which is why the essay was so maddening.

Beth transferred universities long before she graduated, and within a couple of years she had come out as a lesbian. She married her lover, is now covered in tattoos, and sings lead for a piddly band that gets painfully brutal reviews. She got ahold of me a few years ago, told me that she knows it wasn't the best year of her life but that I'd be glad to know she's now healthy and happy. While I'm usually willing to be the bigger person and respect water that can be considered under the bridge, I haven't felt the need to communicate with her. So much for being a Christian, I guess, but I'm still pissed.

I didn't want to keep the little amethyst ring, so I took it to a jewelry store when I went home that summer. The people at Carlton Jewelers would have surely asked questions, and since I didn't really feel like telling them that I'd gotten it for my crazy roommate to keep her from killing herself even though she's now falsely accusing me of being gay, I took the ring to a competitor. He offered me ten bucks for the gold, which, inexplicably, seemed more than fair.

French

Whenever I go home to Oregon to visit, I always stop by Carlton Jewelers. Like I've said, it's probably a classic case of them meaning much more to me than I ever did to them, but what they'll most likely never realize is how much I cherished my time there. Not only was it my first "real" job, aside from helping at my dad's clinic and the assortment of odd jobs I had in college, but it was also a way for me to officially become a part of the jewelry industry. However brief and lowly, I was in like Flynn. The gems, the cases, the velvet boxes. They lit me all up.

When Steve decided to close the Taber Glen store and focus solely on the nicer, newer store in Pinetell, the Taber Glen store manager, Cindy, was assimilated into the Pinetell staff. She and Nancy were good friends, and the two of them were excellent together in the store. And I really mean that. In terms of knowing their clientele and their inventory, I always felt—and still do—in such capable hands when looking for something to buy.

At some point while chatting with Cindy and Nancy, Steve will come out of his workshop and see me and smile.

With his apron and jeweler's goggles on, he'll embrace me in a big hug and then show me whatever piece he's just finished or take me up to his desk and show me a piece with a rare colored stone that he's in the middle of appraising. He takes great pride in knowing that I'm doing well and that I still love jewelry, and while there's usually an instant where I feel like we—me and Carlton Jewelers—are momentarily even on the "what you mean to me" spectrum, I usually leave the store with a pesky fear that they won't even think of me again until the next time I visit.

In addition to catching up with Steve and his staff, the other reason I come to Carlton Jewelers each time I'm home is to buy myself a treat. It's usually Christmastime and I tell myself that I deserve it. It's been a hard/long/eventful/successful year. Whatever kind of year it's been, the point is, it's over, and I deserve a treat. Incidentally, I use a variation of this same argument every time I'm at Tiffany & Co.—although those arguments have less to do with the time of year and more to do with the fact that I am incapable of leaving New York City without a little blue bag.

At some point recently, my dad caught on to my Carlton Jewelers Christmas runs. Remember what I said about jewelry being the ultimate gift idea for women? Maximum reaction with minimum effort? Well, Dad is no fool, and with me already going to the store at Christmastime, that simplified things even further. A couple of years ago when I was home for Christmas and getting ready to head to Carlton's, he told me about a pair of earrings he had seen there. Something about how they were two-toned and reversible, and when it was obvious that his description did not give me a clear picture of what to look for, he drew a little sketch of some circular drop earrings. My instructions were to buy the earrings and he would reimburse me.

The salesperson in me takes these kinds of situations very seriously. Anytime someone expresses interest in having something that I have the ability to provide for them or connect them with, I latch on very tightly. To the point where if anything surfaces that could prevent me from providing what is needed, I will 1) become panicked and sad at the thought of not delivering, and then 2) exhaust every possible option until I have found a way to deliver. This is why sales is such a good fit for me. Because I will do anything in my (or anyone else's) power to get my customers what they need.

The panicked and sad feeling struck me when I got to Carlton's and couldn't find the earrings. I tried to describe them to Cindy, and even using Dad's bizarre verbage, she knew exactly what pair I was talking about and even remembered the day he had come into the store and seen them. She also remembered that they had recently been purchased. Since I couldn't get the pair he wanted, the logical next best thing seemed to be to find another pair of two-toned earrings from the same display. But none of them were drops. None of them were hoops even. The only two-tones were a pair of smallish gold balls, and I didn't like them.

So I called Dad. I described some of the other pairs in the display, and he ultimately told me to just pick out something that I thought was nice, something that Mom would like. I knew Mom would be delighted to get almost anything from a jewelry store, but I decided to go with hoops since they seemed closer to Dad's original idea than anything else. I selected a gold pair, bigger than what she typically wears but not *too* big, and they had some pretty, almost etch-like markings on them that made them unique. Just like the two-tone would have. The etched designs gave the earrings a softer shine, and Dad seemed pleased enough when I brought them home.

When Mom opened them, she was surprised. Dad almost never buys her jewelry, but more than that, he had already given her his gift: A pair of rain boots. (I guess this is what happens when you've been married for over thirty years.) Mom had picked them out, so having the boots wrapped and under the tree for her to open seemed silly. But having her already know what was inside made his insertion of the little jewelry box into the toe of one of the boots a pretty dynamite move. I'd been there when he wrapped the boots, and he was sniggering like a little boy at his own cleverness.

My angel mother insisted she loved the earrings, but she would have said that even if she hadn't, so Dad told her she was welcome to exchange them for something else. I could tell she was thinking about it, if only for a second, but she brushed it away.

"No, I want *these*. It means a lot knowing these are the ones you picked out."

Silence.

More silence.

Mom noticed.

"Unless you just told the ladies there to pick something out for you," Mom said as she turned to Dad, waiting for an answer.

I know what you're thinking, and it was horrible of us to lie to her, but what were we supposed to do? To be honest, I don't even remember what we said, I just remember trying to make it clear that it had been all Dad. Which as far as the idea and the money behind the idea, it *had* been.

The next year it happened again, only this time I had already returned from Carlton's with my Christmas purchase. I'd gotten a pair of gray freshwater pearl drop earrings (this was prior to my disenchantment with pearls), and Dad asked me later that night if they had any more of them in stock. I called the store, and Cindy told me they didn't, but that they could have some ordered in. Since they wouldn't arrive in time for Christmas, I asked her to describe all the pearl earrings they had in stock. Colors, sizes, prices, etc. I presented Dad with a whole slew of options, and he ended up selecting some good-sized black pearl studs. I called Cindy back and told her that my Dad would be picking them up the following day.

This time when Mom opened the box, she may have been a little suspicious already, because her questioning was more specific.

"You actually went to the store?" she asked Dad.

"Yes, I went to the store," he said, and he wasn't lying. He had, after all, picked them up.

In the case of the black pearls, Mom actually did go back to Carlton's to see if there were any other pearls she liked better, but she ended up sticking with the ones Dad and I had picked out, even though neither of us had actually seen them.

I don't mean to throw my Dad under the bus, because there's nothing wrong with having your jewelry-loving daughter who is already going to the jewelry store anyway and has great taste pick out a gift for your wife when your original idea falls through or has already been purchased by someone else. And I stand by that. Besides, any man who would attempt a sketch of circular, two-tone drop earrings is clearly good people.

Point

A woman who used to work at my dad's office once told me that when she died, she wanted to be wrapped in a quilt and buried in her backyard. It was a shocking thing to hear as a youngster, if for no other reason than I'd never heard someone speak about death so unceremoniously.

Contrast this with the typical way that death is handled. Wake, funeral, and graveside services have been held for almost everyone close to me who has died. I think back on my maternal grandmother's funeral frequently, as it was probably the saddest thing my seventeen-year-old self had ever dealt with. The church was overflowing with funeral guests, and her casket was a light shade of pink. Someone told me that they don't actually lower the body into the grave until all the guests have left, and so I couldn't stop myself from turning around and looking out the back window of the car as we drove away from the cemetery. I wanted to see it, I guess because I really *didn't* want to see it. Like an accident you pass by, you stare in spite of yourself. All I knew was that my grandma was being lowered into the earth, and it just seemed like someone ought to see it happen.

It's not that all this pomp is unnecessary. In fact, it's more than warranted. It's more than appropriate. It is in many ways imperative for us to pay our respects and memorialize our loved ones in the most official and grand ways possible. They deserve nothing less.

The reason I even mention this here is that death

has more to do with jewelry than you might think. I suppose it starts with this whole idea of a wedding ring. It, the ring, symbolizes the marriage, and marriage is until death. A rather morbid way of looking at it, but these are just the facts. And when I hear about someone who has died, my thoughts drift toward the ring. Not right away, of course, for I'm nothing if not sentimental, but after the tears, the anger, the grief, the loneliness, the despair, and the soul-searching, I do think about the ring and the life its wearer left behind.

And as long as we're talking about being left behind, that's another thing about jewelry. You can't take it with you. So another way that death involves itself with jewelry is the transfer of ownership that ensues when a jewelry owner passes away. Jewelry—wedding rings in particular—tend to be passed down to the closest surviving female relative. A daughter usually, perhaps a granddaughter or niece in some situations.

I would imagine that the older of my dad's younger sisters now has my grandmother's wedding ring, and it's sad that I don't actually remember this ring at all. I was a very young child during the years we lived in close proximity to her and consequently never thought enough about her ring to study it. We didn't see her much in the years after we moved to Oregon, and when she died, I could not have even told you if her wedding ring was set in white gold or yellow. Far eclipsing this, however, was that I could not have even told you one single thing about *her*. At least her pre-Grandma life. Sitting in the pew listening to the funeral speakers, I couldn't believe what they were saying. The things my grandma had done, what she'd been through, the strength she'd had. I was in awe of her and completely broken hearted that I had missed the chance to know her for myself.

So, admittedly, her ring wasn't on my mind then, but I've thought about it a lot since. And even though it doesn't really mean anything and it wouldn't make up for the time I didn't spend with her, I still feel a slight pull toward whatever jewelry box in California houses the ring she wore for all those decades. Some surround themselves with pedigree charts or old photos to feel connected to previous generations, but I find the jewelry they owned to be much more personal; particularly the wedding rings they wore through it all.

There is a final way that death is tied to jewelry. More so than wills and ownership and marriage symbols, this grand finale is the ultimate connection and involves what just might be my most shocking (and personal) confession.

A relatively new capability in this world, there is actually a way to use human remains in the process of creating a diamond. We're talking synthetic diamonds obviously, but remember that synthetic diamonds can still be chemically identical to those grown in the earth. Memorial diamonds, as they are called, are the real thing. Just grown from the hair or ashes of a deceased person.

Now, I can't tell you how many people crinkle their nose in disgust over hearing about such a thing, and this intrigues me. It *baffles* me. I guess it's the idea of wearing a relative around one's neck that is so bothersome, but to these people, my rebuttal is that I'm not sure urns of ashes displayed on mantles are any less disgusting. On the contrary, they are much more so. Not to mention completely useless.

Personally, I can't think of a more treasured way to preserve someone close to me, and my final confession is that this is how I'd want to go. This is what I want done. As controversial and disturbing as many seem to find it, I can think of no greater way to lay my body to rest. Yes, it's because nothing is more beautiful and precious to me than a diamond, but it's also because such a diamond would be the ultimate heirloom. A literal piece of family history to pass down. And I like thinking about a daughter carrying me with her always, especially after she's read this book and knows how fascinated I always was by the brilliance of a gemstone.

Ashes to ashes, people. Dust to dust. We all end up that way, no matter how we get there. I think of my grandma and my cousin Brian in their caskets below the earth, decomposition having had its way with them. I think of my great-grandmother who chose cremation. I can still see the urn displayed in the center of the funeral service, and I remember thinking it was a pretty bad-ass choice for a ninety-year-old. And then there's my dad's former employee, the one with a quilt and a corner of her backyard picked out. To each his own is my point, and if a person's wishes in this regard are at all a reflection of her personality, then I'd say mine are just about perfect. I always did love sparkles.

up there in
lights i'll be

I'D BEEN SIXTEEN WHEN—AFTER SPENDING the day watching Steve size rings in the workshop of his store—I decided that there was nothing I would rather do in this world than be a jeweler. But in the twelve years that followed, I was busy doing other things that did not involve becoming a jeweler. I earned three degrees, chalked up several years of work experience, and ultimately found myself with a budding career in the thick of corporate America.

Two years into my post-MBA corporate gig, I began to lose steam. Although it wasn't so much a gradual process as it was a sudden revelation while sitting in an all-day meeting that was literally sucking away my will to live. As I looked around the conference room table, it wasn't just that I was horribly uninterested in the subject matter. It was also that everyone else in the room appeared to be fully engaged, interested, *excited.* Even the newly-matriculated college graduate sitting across from me who knew almost nothing about our company or business was abuzz with a combination of questions and insights and suggestions. Truth be told, he was making me look bad, and I should have been furious, but instead of outdoing him with some MBA-level insights, the only action for which I could scrape together the motivation was that of repeatedly raising my head to check the time on the wall clock.

That's when it hit me. This revelation. This epiphany that at the time seemed to be the only thing that could save me from forty more years of suckfest meetings like the one I was in at that moment. "You don't *have* to work in business," a voice seemed to say in my head. Add to this that I was at the time reading a delightful little book called *The Alchemist*, and before the week was out, the dream of being a jeweler had been officially resurrected.

This is probably making it sound like I was regretting having earned my MBA in the first place, or that my entire foray into the corporate world had all been a big mistake. Which, let me be perfectly clear, was not the case. Because what I'm not telling you is that the first two years after my MBA were some of the best of my life. In what was perhaps the perfect job for me, I spent those two years in constant awe of my own luck for having scored a position that made me literally love coming to work. Sometimes I actually felt so satisfied and content in the workforce that it made me want to cry. Though this flirts dangerously with being bat-shit crazy, it doesn't make it any less true. I was in love with my job.

But after two years I took a promotion of sorts, and, always such a crapshoot, this particular promotion didn't turn out to be all that I had hoped it would, and I suddenly found myself in a job I didn't like. My new role was not only terribly uninspiring but it also completely under-leveraged my strengths and skill set. As I calculated the odds of future promotions putting me back within the small niche of business that I actually enjoyed, they didn't look good. I wanted out.

And so I called Steve.

"I want to talk jewelry," I told him.

Steve had always known of my interest in pursuing jewelry, but I'm pretty sure my call took him by surprise. We talked for quite a while, mostly about my jewelry goals, which were albeit hard to pinpoint because I hardly even knew them myself. In fact, I hadn't a clue as to what the world of gemology had to offer me or what exactly was the best way to incorporate it into my career. But Steve offered valuable insight into everything from the business in general to the gemology program that he most recommended.

And then a strange thing happened.

It's not that I actually *asked* if I could buy his store, but in the course of the conversation, I heard myself ask what his sixty-eight-year-old self was planning to do with it. He replied that since neither of his sons wanted to take over the business, he planned on having a blow-out going out of business sale when he was ready to retire, which, according to my calculations, could have happened as early as the very next day.

"Unless *Tali* wants to buy my store," he threw out.

While it was nothing more than an abstract pipe dream of mine at that point, we still talked at length about the possibility, and suddenly my MBA seemed as valuable as ever. Paired with a gemology degree, wouldn't that set me up nicely to run my own store? Wouldn't coming back to my beloved Oregon be ideal?

Of course, the potential price he threw out was the sort of number that could make the weak-hearted immediately crap their pants. My intestines have always been questionable, so crapping was not outside the realm of possibility as we continued to talk and my bowels continued to churn every time the word "million" was spoken by either of us.

"But I'm not ready to retire yet," Steve said as we wrapped up our call.

"Well, I'm not ready to be a jeweler yet," I answered.

"Call me when you are," Steve said, perfectly sincere, and I made a note to do just that.

I then ran straight to the bathroom.

Long octagon

My second trip to Tiffany & Co.'s flagship store in New York City came seven years after my first. Pushing thirty by this time, I'd lived a lot of life in those seven years. Much had changed, most notably my employer. The first time I'd come to the city, my newly-matriculated self worked for a small logistics company. As an account manager, I loved the work I did. I loved the clients, I loved making their lives easier, I loved being their girl. What I didn't love was my salary, which even after three years of service was still barely breaking $25K. As a college graduate, I was slightly pissed. And as a kick-ass employee who not only gave everything I had to that job but also had my accounts eating out of the palm of my hand, I was *majorly* pissed. And while I cried like a baby when I quit that job, going back to school was the best financial decision I've ever made. Even on my internship—my *internship*—I was making more than triple the money I had as an underpaid account manager.

This second trip to Tiffany saw me working for a Fortune 500 Company, and while my enthusiasm for business was fading, my salary was growing, and it was a far cry from the world of time clocks, overtime, and hourly wages; a world that would have never produced the cash needed to fund my jewelry degree. That was the whole reason I was back in New York in the first place. Because my conversation with Steve had inspired me to get serious about this particular dream. Clearly, if anything was bat-shit crazy, it was the idea of me buying a seven-figure jewelry business. Yet there it was. Stretched before me just like little Santiago's treasure, for if anything in this world could qualify as my personal calling, it had to be jewelry.

In all honesty, I had no idea if I'd end up buying Steve's store or even if I wanted to. It would mean spending my career in a small town; a town hit hard by the economic downturn and not likely to ever fully recover. It would mean borrowing an insane amount of money in said small town and putting all my eggs in one basket. A very sparkly basket, mind you, but a singular basket nonetheless. It would mean parting forever with city life. Sports teams, museums, theater, fine dining, shopping centers. It felt like I'd be giving up a lot. But I'd also be getting one hell of a store. Steve had a phenomenal reputation that had spread county-wide. And his store was one of the most beautiful I'd ever seen. Other than my parents' house, Carlton Jewelers was my favorite place to go when visiting Oregon, and owning it would in many ways be my ultimate dream fulfilled.

Another decision for another day, but first things

first. Because to even have the *option* of becoming a jeweler or incorporating jewelry into my career on any level, I needed to be able to do more than ogle its beauty from the other side of the display case. And so I enrolled in the prestigious Graduate Gemologist program at the Gemological Institute of America.

So, yeah. A lot of things in my life were different this time around in New York, but there was one glaring similarity between my twenty-two and twenty-nine-year-old selves: I was still more excited about visiting Tiffany & Co. than I was about any other attraction in the city.

Again wishing to purchase a small memento, I found myself on the crowded silver floor. I was enchanted with Tiffany's trendy line of key necklaces, and after ruling out the platinum and gold versions on the first floor, I was pleased to see some identical-looking silver versions in one of the front cases. I picked my favorite — it had an almost wheel-looking key base with a small diamond in the center — and compared it to a few other necklaces as I perused the rest of the cases. The key necklace was the most expensive one I had selected, but having learned my lesson the last time I was in this predicament, I bought it anyway. And then, naturally, I went to look at engagement rings.

My preferences having shifted away from the two-carat solitaires that used to have me so captivated, I was no longer interested in a particular "type" of ring. I couldn't explain what I liked, but I knew it when I saw it. And so it took a surprisingly short amount of time for me to sweep the floor and pick out the best ring. There were two of them, one of a slightly smaller scale than the other, but both bearing an ovalish stone surrounded by two halos of baby rounds. The style almost looked antique, and I loved how the shape was sort of in between cuts. More oblong than a round brilliant, but more squat than an oval.

I thought of my mother for a split second as I debated back and forth between the smaller stone and the bigger stone, but who was I kidding? The ring with the bigger stone was clearly the better choice. Not that there was anything to choose. I wasn't in the market. I was simply in town.

Glancing down at the price tag, I was shocked to see my new favorite was selling for only $11,000. This seemed downright cheap compared to my $32,000 pick seven years before.

Someone really ought to snatch me up, I thought.
Before I rediscover solitaires.

Shield

I wasn't sure what to wear on my first day of jewelry school. It was New York City, the streets were constantly crowded with well-dressed professionals, and I really wanted to look the part. On the other hand, I didn't want to walk from my rented Times Square apartment to the campus on Madison Avenue wearing heels. And seeing as how the September air wasn't full of the slight autumn chill I had anticipated, what I really felt like wearing was a tank top and shorts. Damn, it was muggy.

I ended up settling for grey chinos and a dark green shirt with a bit of sparkle on the shoulders. A good halfway point between professional and casual, I figured this would cover me either way. Although it was obvious as soon as I entered the classroom that I had still grossly overdressed. By the last day of class, I had downgraded to a t-shirt, jeans, and Chuck Taylors.

Meant to teach us how to grade colored stones, this particular class became a bit of a mixed bag for me, much of it more distressing than enjoyable. For one thing, there was only one other person besides me who wasn't already in the jewelry business. Which I guess I could have predicted if I'd actually sat down and thought about it, but looking around at all my classmates and hearing about their already lengthy careers in the business, it made me feel foolish. More than that, it made me question whether this was even possible for someone like me. Not just the completion of the degree, but also the career switch I was hoping for after I was done. The girls at the Cleveland corundum seminar had painted a nice picture of possibility, but I was unconvinced.

And through talking with my classmates, most of them much further along in this degree than I was, I learned more about the big final exam required once all your course and lab work was completed. It was a twenty-stone challenge in which you not only had to identify what the stones were, you also had to correctly grade them on everything we were learning in this class and more. And just to give you a frame of reference, we were learning enough in this class to fill out an entire two-sided sheet of paper's worth of information. And that's per stone. The thought of having to do this for twenty stones and not get even one single detail wrong was overwhelming. And learning that the average person in this program ends up taking the final exam six to seven times before passing was more than just depressing. It was show-stopping.

Because what you might not realize is there's a fair amount of subjectivity involved when it comes to grading gemstones. I myself hadn't even realized this until sitting in that colored stone grading class, but the truth is that if you had several gemologists fill out one of these two-sided sheets for a certain stone, their answers would be different. The differences would be slight, but there would be differences. And even as I got better as the class went on, I was never able to get my papers to entirely match what was shown on the answer keys.

Take brilliance, for example. The total brilliance in a colored stone, given as a percentage, is the number you're left with after subtracting the percentages of the stone that show windowing and extinction. A window occurs when, instead of its true color, you see a light and almost see-through area in a stone. If you hold a page of printed text underneath the windowed area of a stone, you'll be able to clearly see and read the text through it. Extinction on the other hand refers to the dark areas on a stone that also fail to show the true color present in a gemstone. They'll show up as almost black. Aside from windowing and extinction, brilliance is everything else; the beautiful flashes of rich color seen on a gemstone.

The slippery thing about determining brilliance is that when grading colored stones, you try and find the angle at which the brilliance is maximized. Stones, after all, do look different from each angle, and even if one angle shows only thirty percent brilliance, if another angle shows fifty, you put the stone down as having fifty percent brilliance. But what are the odds that people will view the same stone the same way? What are the odds that I'm going to agree with you on what the most brilliant angle is in the first place? And what are the odds that even if we picked the same angle we'd both agree on a fifty percent brilliance?

Brilliance was by far the hardest element of the colored stone grading class, such that I found myself approaching the instructor frequently to ask him what I seemed to be missing. My brilliance estimations were always significantly different than those shown on the answer keys, and it always felt like such a stab in the dark. On one particular stone, the windowing shown on the answer key was fifty percent, but I found the stone to be much more brilliant than that. I handed the stone to the instructor, and he agreed with me.

"I'd say it's more like twenty-five percent," he said, which filled me with relief, as twenty-five percent is exactly what I had put on my own paper for the windowing value.

But the relief soon gave way to distress and frustration as the idea of the big final exam became more and more ridiculous. How is zero margin for error even a realistic expectation when subjectivity is in the picture? I wasn't anywhere near being finished with all the course work required for the degree, but one of the takeaways from my colored stones class was that passing the big final seemed impossible.

Despite the heavy dose of reality that overcame me in the colored stones classroom, it was still one of the best experiences of my life up to that point. Because no matter how hard earning this degree was going to be, I loved that I was doing it. I loved learning about jewelry. No matter how daunting the final exam, that didn't change the fact that I was spending entire days doing nothing but playing with gems. At my own little station with my own microscope, loupe, and tweezers, I couldn't possibly have been more content.

And on top of that, I got pretty good at grading stones. I'd been given a small oval ruby and a large emerald-cut aquamarine for the test at the end of the class, and I'd gotten an eighty-eight percent on one and a whopping ninety-six percent on the other. When the instructor announced that only a few people had gotten a combined average in the nineties, I realized that I was one of those few; the few who had done better than everyone else. And I wasn't even in the business. Ha! Even a few of my classmates commented to me that they couldn't believe how quickly I had picked things up.

I'd been fishing for compliments when I began sharing the news with friends that I had done well in my first class, but most people just shrugged it off as a no-brainer.

"Of course you did," they'd say. "It's your passion."

And I suppose it is this passion that left me feeling as hopeful and satisfied as ever as my Chuck Taylors took me back to Times Square, colored stone grading certificate in hand. Of course it helped that one of my classmates had, with the completion of this colored stones class, finished her degree. She was now a gemologist, officially, and she'd passed the big final on only her second try. Not one for attention, she was a bit uncomfortable when a campus administrator came into our classroom that last day with a beautiful chocolate cake from a high-end New York City bakery.

"A little birdie told me that someone in this room is our newest Graduate Gemologist," the administrator said as she placed the cake in front of my shy classmate.

This classmate had been through some rough times, both personally and professionally, and she'd been working on this degree for ten years. *Ten years.* I couldn't even imagine, as I was hoping to have it completed in two. Seeing the happiness pouring off of her as we celebrated her achievement filled me with a renewed determination to see this thing through. I wanted that same happiness, that same sense of achievement after all the struggles and self-doubt, that same chocolate cake with my name on it. And when Tiffany & Co. came to campus to recruit, as they had done that very week, I wanted to be able to throw my hat in the ring and drop everything if they called.

acknowledgements

I have my usual team of talented professionals to thank for their assistance with making this book a reality. To Kristin Lindstrom, Victoria Colotta, and Madison Jones, my sincere thanks for your time and talents.

I must also thank a certain jewelry store, the one I mention throughout this book, because it is this jewelry store to whom I feel I owe the biggest amount of thanks. As I learned from my first book, nothing damages relationships faster than writing about people, but my hope is that the love I have for this beautiful store is what shines through these pages. Truly no one has had a bigger influence or shown as much support when it comes to my pursuit of gemology, and to this jeweler, his wife, and his staff, I will be forever grateful.

about the author

Tali Nay, whose first book, *Schooled*, chronicled her journey through the education system, has somehow managed to find herself back in a classroom. She is currently pursuing a Graduate Gemology degree. It's taking longer than planned, but anything worth having is not easy to get. At least that's what she tells herself when studying mine locations and chemical composi- tions late into the night. Tali lives in Cleveland, Ohio, which, in August of 2013, became Tiffany & Co.'s newest store location. Visit www.talinaybooks.com for more information about Tali and her books.

the jewelry

10672514R00154

Made in the USA
San Bernardino, CA
22 April 2014